Beadwork Inspired by Art

ImPressionist

jewelry and accessories

Creative Publishing international

First published in the United States of America by

Creative Publishing international, Inc., a member of
Quayside Publishing Group
400 First Avenue North
Suite 300
Minneapolis, MN 55401
1-800-328-3895
www.creativepub.com

ISBN-13: 978-1-58923-387-4
ISBN-10: 1-58923-387-5

10 9 8 7 6 5 4 3 2 1

Library of Congress Cataloging-in-Publication Data

Campbell, Jean, 1964-

 Beadwork inspired by art : Impressionist jewelry and accessories / by Jean Campbell and Judith Durant.

 p. cm.

 Includes index.

 ISBN 1-58923-387-5

 1. Beadwork. 2. Impressionism (Art) I. Durant, Judith, 1955- II. Title.

 TT860.C35746 2008

 745.594'2--dc22

 2008010476

Cover and Book Design: Everlution Design
Page Layout: Everlution Design
Illustrations: Julia S. Pretl
Photography: Glenn Scott Photography
Cover Image: *Landscape with Carriage and Train* (Scala/Art Resource, NY)
Copy Editor: Amy Fletcher
Proofreader: Karen C. Ruth

Printed in Singapore

Beadwork Inspired by Art

Impressionist

jewelry and accessories

JEAN CAMPBELL & JUDITH DURANT

Creative Publishing
international

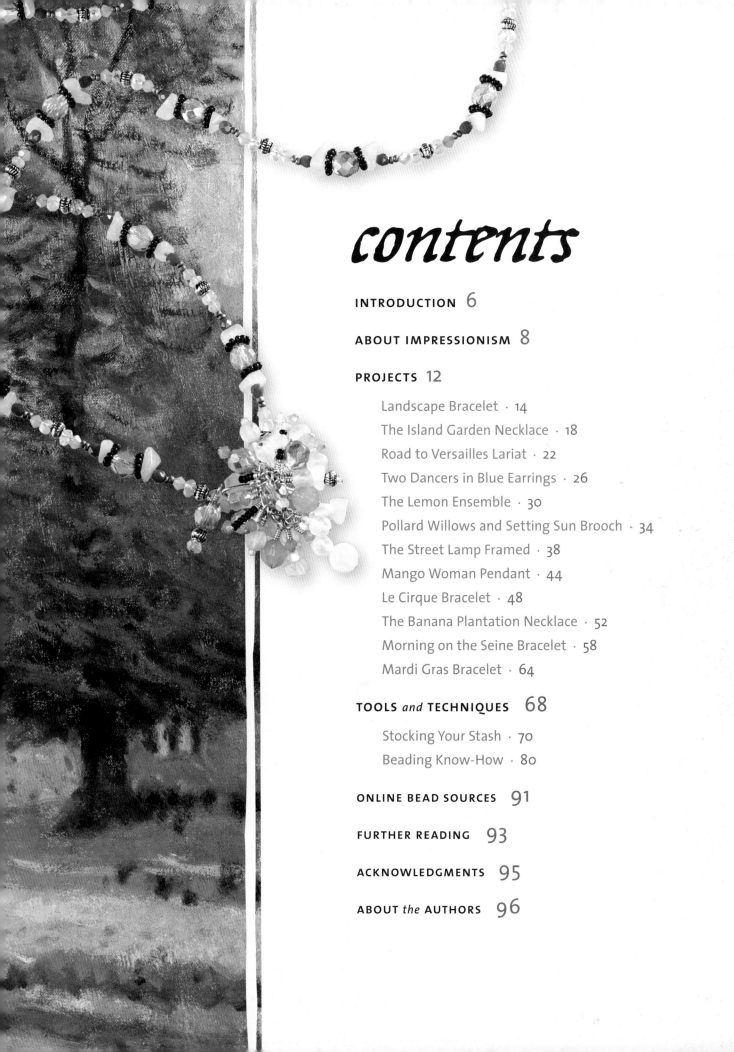

contents

introduction

INSPIRED BY THE GREAT MASTERPIECES of fine
artists—and working with a vast array of beads
and numerous techniques from stringing to
weaving—beadworkers can produce their
own works of art. A fine artist might work with
paint and canvas while a beadworker "paints"
with beads and thread, but both use color,
texture, and design to create unique works of art.

As beadworkers ourselves, we're both always hungry
to learn more ways to work with color and texture. So we
decided to look to the masters for inspiration. In *Beadwork Inspired by Art: Impressionist Jewelry and Accessories*, we explore the
unique painting style that began with a small circle of French painters
who were un-impressed with the static style of painting that was *la mode*
(the style) in Europe during the 1860s.

The Impressionist style of painting offers great opportunities to work with color.
In many paintings of this genre, artists applied small amounts of color next to small
amounts of another color, rather than mixing them. A beadworker can easily imitate this effect with several
colors of beads. We picked some of our favorite Impressionist works, spent time with them at home and
at the bead store, and let them be our muses as we designed the twelve projects you'll find in this book.

We discovered that just as there are many ways to interpret a sunset, a still life, or a flight of imagination
into a work of art, so are there many ways to interpret a work of art into beadwork. We took a somewhat
literal approach to recreating a painting for *The Street Lamp Framed* on page 38. We focused on color and
texture for *Le Cirque Bracelet* on page 48 and *The Banana Plantation Necklace* on page 52. The interpretation
of mood and color also led us to create *Road to Versailles Lariat* on page 22 and *Mardi Gras Bracelet* on page 64.

As you flip through the book, you'll find clear step-by-step instructions to make each design. The detailed
illustrations will help you get the job done, too. If you're new to a technique or are maybe a little rusty, check
pages 80–89 for all the background information you'll need to know.

We hope that by creating these projects, you'll learn a little more about how to work with color and texture
in your own designs. And wearing beadwork inspired by a work of art is a conversation just waiting to happen!
Who knows? You may soon be paging through art books yourself and finding inspiration for your own
beaded masterpieces.

about impressionism

Impressionism is the name given to an art movement that began in Paris in the 1860s. Paintings in this style are known for their loose strokes of color, which are applied side by side. The brushstrokes—short, choppy, broad, or sometimes a series of dots—created an "impression" and left the color mixing to the eye of the beholder. This new style of painting was in direct contrast to the classic, realistic styles of French painting popular at the time. Coupled with the fact that the artists worked outside the studio, amid nature—*en plein air* (outdoors)—Impressionism did anything but impress the art critics or art collectors of the time.

The painting that brought the movement to the public's attention was Claude Monet's *Impression, Sunrise* (1872). The scene is a harbor view from the artist's window in Le Havre, France. The foggy image depicts small dinghies in the foreground and monstrous ships and smokestacks on the horizon. The sky and water become one as misty grays and blues mix with oranges and whites. The sun, a bright orange dot, pierces the mist. Monet used the same type of broad brushstrokes to paint the waves, the boats, and the smokestacks. The balanced composition is made up mainly of abstract shifts in color.

Monet exhibited his painting in 1874 at a photographer's gallery. Critic Louis Leroy lambasted Monet and his "impressionist school" as an outrageous experiment. Unwittingly, Leroy coined the term for the art movement that would later be revered. At the time, however, many considered this relaxed, modern style, which had already been developing for at least a decade, a radical attack on the great traditions of art and France.

The artists known as the Impressionists—Claude Monet, Edouard Manet, Alfred Sisley, Pierre Auguste Renoir, Paul Cézanne, Edgar Degas, Mary Cassatt, Georges Seurat, Vincent van Gogh, Paul Gauguin, and many others—were intrigued by the movements of nature: the rising and setting sun, drifting clouds, rippling water. They also closely studied the process of a person's change in pose or expression. Painting was a means by which they could convey intuitive impulses, fleeting feelings, or physical sensations. These artists were more interested in a personal view of the world than in a precise and well-formulated one. They even applied their theories to still-life paintings, animating the inanimate. By adding their humanity to their work, they felt they could transcend the flat canvas and reveal art's truth and purity. Art critics found it hard to accept this new, radical theory.

Although these ideas are common among modern artists, transcendence was certainly not a goal among most of the artists of the time. Tradition, technique, and salability were more important considerations. These painters created grand, often mythical images of heroes and heroines. With color, light, and setting, the subjects of these paintings were dramatically staged, as if they were in a photo studio. The classic technique of realistic perspective held no surprises.

These traditional artists held an important place in society both because of how they painted and what their paintings depicted. Their style of painting appealed to the wealthy middle class, who were also often the subjects of portraits. The Impressionists, however, did not cater to this audience. As a result, the press, the art

Impression, Sunrise

The press coined the term *Impressionism* in 1874 after Claude Monet exhibited this painting, entitled *Impression, Sunrise*. All the colors and shapes in this painting, painted in 1872, fuse together to portray nature's tranquility, even among the likely noise of the ships and smokestacks.

(RÉUNION DES MUSÉES NATIONAUX / ART RESOURCE, NY)

galleries, and the general public of rejected the Impressionists' work, which was so different from the Renaissance-style paintings that had dominated the art world for centuries.

The simplest way to distinguish the two artistic styles is in terms of imagination. Whereas traditional painters stuck to a certain manner of style and representation, the Impressionists took great creative leaps. For the Impressionists, the sky was not always blue, the sun didn't always shine from above, and fabled warriors and people of high social status weren't the only individuals worthy of portraits.

The Impressionists worked with color in a way that reflected how they personally saw the world. Mary Cassatt's portraits are a great example. In *Portrait of Lydia Cassatt* (1880), the mostly staid figure is draped in a wildly colored wrap that seems to meld into the bench on which she sits. The bench then blends with the natural colors of the background, so all are a blur of color. Cassatt chose to paint her sister's face with traditional flesh tones. This area is the first place one looks when viewing the portrait, thus revealing its importance and Cassatt's feelings about the sitter.

Another key element of Impressionism is the technique of painting with very visible brushstrokes. Renoir's *Dance at Bougival* (1883) shows a couple engaged in a lively dance. The background is painted with bold, diagonal strokes to suggest the spinning couple's view of the scene. The whirl of the woman's dress is a flurry of brushstrokes and the details of her lace trimmings are blurred, just as they would be if one were watching the dance.

The Starry Night

Vincent van Gogh's *The Starry Night* is one of the most well-known paintings of the Impressionist movement. It depicts a sky of wondrous celestials and, true to the style, is full of motion and feeling. It was painted in 1889.

(*Digital Image © The Museum of Modern Art /Licensed by Scala / Art Resource, NY*)

The way the Impressionists portrayed perspective was also a departure from the past. Degas was especially experimental in this regard. In *Green Dancer* (1880), he depicts a ballet rehearsal. A line of dancers, wearing red, rests along a wall while green-tutu-wearing ballerinas dance in the center of the floor. The viewer looks at the scene from above, so the horizon line is indistinct. Almost one-third of the painting is the floor, which seems to curve down in an unreal fashion. These shifts in perspective were all blatant rule-breakers of the established academic style.

Van Gogh clearly illustrates many of the tenets of Impressionism in his painting *The Starry Night* (1889). A swirling sky of firework-like stars and a cartoonish moon hang over rolling hills. A small town is tucked neatly at the bottom of the painting. Even though this is a night scene, there is riot of color—vibrant blues,

purples, greens, and yellows. The swirls and other shapes are primarily created with the same type of brushstroke—choppy, short lines of solid color that combine to give shape to the scene. The subject of this painting is nature—the heavenly orbs above, a large cypress tree below. The inhabited town in the foothills, created with traditional perspective, is not prominent, but rather simply part of the landscape. In contrast, the elements with slightly warped perspective, such as the larger-than-real moon and sparklier-than-normal stars, give the whole piece a dreamlike appearance. These elements exemplify Van Gogh's view that nature is full of wonders.

Dozens of important artists contributed to the beginnings of the Impressionist movement. Manet was a huge influence on Monet, Cézanne, and Renoir, and painted early Impressionist-style paintings, such as *Luncheon on the Grass* (1863). Sisley worked with Monet and Renoir to challenge formal painting, using loose lines and color combinations to portray nature scenes in paintings such as *Promenade* (1890). Cézanne, well known for his paintings of fruit and draped fabric, created freeform planes that let the images "emerge" from the canvas, as in *Still Life with Flowered Curtain* (1900–1906). Seurat experimented with small dots of color, relying on the pixilation to mix the colors in the viewers' eyes in paintings such as *Sunday Afternoon on the Island of La Grande Jatte* (1885–1886). Gauguin, who was greatly influenced by Japanese woodblock prints, created the same type of simple composition and pure, but often unrealistic, color forms to create his fantastical images, such as those in *The Yellow Christ* (1889).

Because of their radical approach, the Impressionists were considered outsiders, freaks. They weren't invited to exhibit at the Salon, the official French art exhibition, or to become part of the French Academy of Art. Because of their desire for a higher artistic truth, their propensity for self-imposed exile, and their willingness to sacrifice all for their art, the Impressionists were, in a sense, the first of the beatniks—the rebellious bohemian artists that created the Beat movement of the 1950s. Traditional painters always had exhibitions, commissions, and patrons, so the idea of the "starving artist" was a new one in these times.

Although most Impressionists lived ascetic lifestyles and didn't sell many paintings during their lifetimes, they were passionate about what they were doing and pursued their art on a more spiritual level. These artists considered themselves to be members of a new type of religious order. As Cézanne put it, "Art is a priesthood which requires pure souls who belong to it entirely."

INSPIRING ARTISTS *of the* IMPRESSIONIST MOVEMENT

EMILE BERNARD *(1868–1941)*

PIERRE BONNARD *(1867–1947)*

MARY CASSATT *(1844–1926)*

PAUL CÉZANNE *(1839–1906)*

JEAN-BAPTISTE CAMILLE COROT *(1796–1875)*

GUSTAVE COURBET *(1819–1877)*

EDGAR DEGAS *(1834–1917)*

PAUL GAUGUIN *(1848–1903)*

CORNELIO GERANZANI *(1880–1955)*

CHILDE HASSAM *(1859–1935)*

EDOUARD MANET *(1832–1883)*

CLAUDE MONET *(1840–1926)*

HENRY MORET *(1856–1913)*

BERTHE MORISOT *(1841–1895)*

CAMILLE PISSARRO *(1830–1903)*

PIERRE AUGUSTE RENOIR *(1841–1919)*

GEORGES SEURAT *(1859–1891)*

PAUL SIGNAC *(1863–1935)*

ALFRED SISLEY *(1839–1899)*

HENRI DE TOULOUSE-LAUTREC *(1864–1901)*

VINCENT VAN GOGH *(1853–1890)*

EDOUARD VUILLARD *(1868–1940)*

JAMES ABBOTT MCNEILL WHISTLER *(1834–1903)*

projects

Landscape Bracelet

Landscape with Carriage and Train

Vincent van Gogh, one of the most popular Impressionists, painted *Landscape with Carriage and Train* in 1890, one month before he took his own life. Plagued with chronic depression, he was under the care of a doctor named Paul Gauchet in Auvers-sur-Oise, France, at the time. Van Gogh was a feverish correspondent and wrote hundreds of letters. In a letter to his mother about this series of landscapes, he wrote, "I am quite absorbed in the endless sea of wheat fields set against the hills of gentle yellow and delicate green and violet ploughed earth, regularly checkered with potato plants in flower under a sky of blue, white, pink, and violet."

(SCALA / ART RESOURCE, NY)

VINCENT VAN GOGH'S *Landscape with Carriage and Train* is made up of fairly uniform geometric shapes, but the painting is anything but static. With his energetic brushstrokes and thick, textural application of color, the artist expresses the feeling of a light breeze, the sounds of nature mingled with a distant train, and the earthy scent of healthy farmlands. This colorful peyote-stitched bracelet does the same, including squares as part of the design but making the shapes freeform and alive with color.

FINISHED LENGTH:

6⅝" (17 cm)

TECHNIQUES:

peyote stitch, stringing

MATERIALS AND TOOLS

· size 6° seed beads: 7 g teal-lined transparent topaz

· size 9° three-cut seed beads, 5 g blue iris

· size 8° cylinder beads: 5 g shiny white, 5 g gunmetal

· size 11° seed beads: 5 g transparent crystal, 5 g shiny gold, 5 g lime green rainbow

· 3mm Japanese drop beads (28 to 32), lime green

· 4mm crystal bicones (22 to 26), dark red

· ³/₁₆" x 1" (5 mm x 2.5 cm) sterling silver 5-hole box clasp (1)

· 2½" (6.5 cm) French wire, gold

· 6-lb. test braided beading thread

· scissors

· size 12 beading needle

1 Cut the French wire into ten ¼" (6 mm) pieces. Set aside.

2 Thread the needle with 3' (1 m) of thread. Leaving a 4" (10 cm) tail, pick up eight 6° beads. Use a mix of cylinder and drop beads to work peyote stitch across the initial strand. Use two 11° cylinder beads, one 11° cylinder bead and one drop, or one 8° cylinder bead in each stitch (**figure 1**).

figure 1

As you work, keep the design random, occasionally departing to form stripes like those in the painting. Make sure to add the drops so they all sit on the front of the square. Work twenty-four rows in all. Use 6° beads for two more rows to match the first two rows. Secure the thread and trim it close to the work. Set aside the square.

3 Repeat step 2 to make five more beaded squares. (For a longer bracelet, make six more squares.)

4 Start a new thread that exits from an end bead of the third row of one of the beaded squares. Pass the needle through the hollow center of one of the French wire segments and the first loop on one half of the clasp. Pass back through the bead just exited and tighten to pull the French wire into a loop. Weave through the beads on the same edge of the square in order to exit from a bead opposite the next clasp loop (**figure 2**).

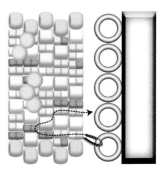

figure 2

Repeat to connect the beaded square to the remaining loops of the clasp half. Secure the thread and trim it close to the work.

5 Repeat step 4 using a new beaded square and the other half of the clasp.

6 Start a new thread on one of the beaded squares that have a clasp half attached. Weave through the beads so the thread exits from an end bead of the third or fourth row opposite the clasp. Pick up one crystal and pass through the matching edge bead of a second beaded square (one with no clasp attached). Weave through the edge beads and exit a few rows up from where you added the last crystal. Pick up one crystal and pass through the matching edge bead of the first beaded square **(figure 3)**.

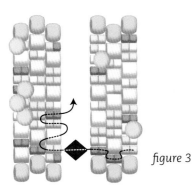

figure 3

Continue working this way, connecting the two squares together with four to six crystals. Add the crystals in a random fashion to keep the freeform look of the beaded squares. Reinforce the connection by weaving through the beads again **(figure 4)**.

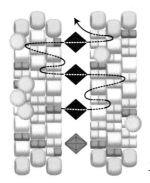

figure 4

7 Repeat step 6 to attach the second beaded square to a third, the third to a fourth, the fourth to a fifth, and the fifth to the remaining square with the attached clasp half.

WORKING WITH COLOR

The Impressionists worked with strokes of color to create an overall effect. You can do the same by creating an Impressionist palette of bead colors. Choose the colors you'd like to use for your project. Then gather together the tubes and bags of beads, spill them all into a pile, and mix them up. If your project calls for a completely random palette— perhaps one that conveys color shifts—only occasionally look down at the pile as you pick up beads. For a slightly more structured color palette, as with *Landscape Bracelet*, choose one bead type or color over another as you go to create soft lines or patches of color.

The Island Garden Necklace

The Island Garden

Born in Dorchester, Massachusetts, in 1859, Childe Hassam studied at the Boston Art School and the École des Beaux-Arts in Paris. He was perhaps the most important American Impressionist. *The Island Garden*, painted in 1892, is watercolor on paper.

THIS PAINTING BY Childe Hassam conveys extraordinary lushness and depth while relying on relatively few colors and abstract shapes. The necklace of pearls, cat's eye beads, and seed beads reflects this same depth through the luster of the colors and the dense formation of the spiral.

FINISHED LENGTH:

16" (41 cm) including the clasp

TECHNIQUES:

spiral stitch

MATERIALS AND TOOLS

· size 11° seed beads: 3 g each
  white (A) and pale copper or
  salmon (B)

· 4.5–5mm freshwater oval
  pearls (102), approximately
  24" (61 cm)

· 6mm cat's eye beads (34)

· hook and eye clasp (1),
  sterling silver

· 6-lb. test braided beading thread

· size 13 beading needle

· scissors

1 Thread a needle with approximately 3' (1 m) of thread. Pick up one pearl, one cat's eye, one pearl, two A, three B, one pearl, three B, and two A. Leaving a 6" (15 cm) tail, pass through the first pearl, the cat's eye, and the second pearl again **(figure 1)**.

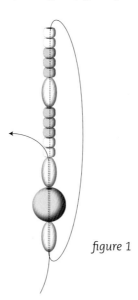

figure 1

2 Pick up one cat's eye, two A, three B, one pearl, three B, and two A. Pass through the cat's eye and the last pearl of the previous set, then pass through the cat's eye just added **(figure 2)**.

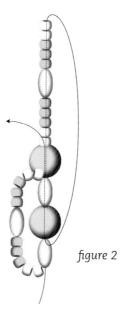

figure 2

3 Pick up one pearl, two A, three B, one pearl, three B, and two A. Pass through the last pearl and cat's eye, then pass through the pearl just added **(figure 3)**.

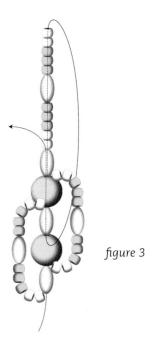

figure 3

Repeat steps 2 and 3 until necklace measures 16" (41 cm) or desired length.

4 Pick up four A and slide one half of the clasp over these beads. Weave back into the last pearl of the necklace, then reinforce the connection by passing through the beads again. Pass the thread down into the beadwork. Tie the thread with a half-hitch knot and weave through several more beads, pulling the thread taut to force the knot inside a bead. Use the tail thread to repeat on the other end. Secure the threads and trim close to the beadwork.

SPIRAL STITCH UP CLOSE

Changing the size, shape, and number of beads in your spiral stitch will produce vastly different results. *The Island Garden Necklace* combines oblong pearls, round cat's eye beads, and seed beads. The core beads are pearls and cat's eye beads, and the outer beads are a combination of pearls and seed beads. The result is a lush spiral of beads with similar prominence.

The first variation shown here begins with a core of two pearls. The outer strands have ten seed beads. Because the core beads are so much larger than the outer strands, the core is most prominent, and the outer beads are accents.

The second variation begins with a core of four 8° seed beads. The outer strands have seven 11° seed beads. Because the beads are closer in size, the spiral is much denser than the other examples. The core and outer beads have about the same visual weight.

The third variation uses 11° seed beads. The core and outer strands all have four beads. The spiral is tight, and the core is almost obscured by the outer beads.

Road to Versailles Lariat

Road to Versailles

Alfred Sisley, Pierre Auguste Renoir, and Claude Monet are the three artists credited for instigating the Impressionist movement. Sisley was a Brit born in Paris in 1839. He moved to London to study business, but Paris's art scene proved to be irresistible and he soon returned. He was a master at painting skies and he studied specific spots in France and England to make his many nature-inspired works. Unfortunately, Sisley, unlike his colleagues, was a horrible salesman, so he spent most of his life in poverty. Shortly before his death of throat cancer at age sixty, he began to gain notoriety among critics and the public.

(Eric Lessing / Art Resource, NY)

THE PAINTING THAT INSPIRED this beaded lariat is a classic Impressionist work that glorifies nature, employs broad brushstrokes, and explores a painting style that allows the viewers' eyes to mix colors and decipher shapes. The beaded lariat is a take on those qualities, with its loose stringing pattern and a palette inspired by nature. The design culminates with a glass cloud that has, quite literally, a silver lining. For a classic look, wear this piece long. For a more contemporary style, wind it around the neck twice.

FINISHED LENGTH:

33½" (85 cm)

TECHNIQUES:

knotting, crimping, wirework

MATERIALS AND TOOLS

- size 11° seed beads, 5 g forest green
- size 11° seed beads (64), olivine
- size 6° triangle beads (6), translucent white
- 4mm crystal bicones (44), light blue opal
- 4mm fire-polished beads (32), carnelian
- 4 x 5mm rondelles (33), semiprecious aquamarine
- 4 x 5mm fancy wide-holed sterling
- silver barrel spacers (19)
- 6mm fire-polished beads (12), translucent white
- 6–8mm lemon semiprecious quartz chips (36)
- 8mm fire-polished beads (20), olivine AB
- 8mm crystal round beads (4), light blue
- 8mm round bead (1), white quartz

- 2 x 2mm sterling silver crimp tubes (2)
- 5mm sterling silver round jump ring (1)
- 22-gauge sterling silver head pins (30), 2" (5 cm)
- 12mm sterling silver fish hook clasp (1)
- 5 x 8mm sterling silver oval chain (7 links)
- 6-lb. test braided beading thread
- fine-width flexible beading wire, 35" (89 cm)
- size 11 sharp needle
- scissors
- wire cutters
- crimping pliers
- chain-nose pliers

1 Thread the needle with a 10" (25.5 cm) length of thread. Leaving a 3" (7.5 cm) tail, pick up ten green seed beads and tie a square knot. Pass through the beads again several times until you have a very firm, tight circle. Secure the thread and trim. Set aside. Repeat to make thirty-two bead rings in all **(figure 1)**.

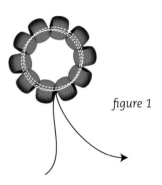

figure 1

2 Cut the chain to make one chain with six links. Set aside the remaining link.

3 Use a crimp tube to attach the beading wire to one end of the six-link chain. String one barrel spacer and let it slide over the crimp. String one aquamarine and one bicone. String a sequence of beads in this order: two olivine seed beads, one carnelian fire-polished, one chip, one bead ring, one green fire-polished, one bead ring, one chip, one carnelian fire-polished, two olivine seed beads, one bicone, one aquamarine, one barrel spacer, one aquamarine, and one bicone. Repeat the sequence fourteen more times.

String two olivine seed beads, one carnelian fire-polished, one chip, one bead ring, one green fire-polished, one bead ring, one chip, one carnelian fire-polished, two olivine seed beads, one bicone, one aquamarine, one crimp tube, one barrel spacer, and the last link. Pass back through the crimp tube, snug the beads, and crimp.

4 Use the remaining beads to embellish the six-link chain with an assortment of dangles. Make the dangles in various lengths, from ½" to 1" (1.5 to 2.5 cm). First string the selected beads onto a head pin. Begin a wrapped loop, but before making the wrap, attach the loop onto one of the links. Make the wrap to secure the dangle. It's best to add longer dangles to the bottom of the chain and shorter ones near the top. Add at least four dangles to each link, making sure you add the dangles to each side of the links **(figure 2)**.

figure 2

5 Add a final dangle to the single link at the other end of the lariat.

6 Use the jump ring to attach the clasp to a middle link on the chain.

MAKE YOUR OWN CLASP

Making your own fish hook clasp is an easy way to personalize your beadwork. Start by cutting and straightening a 2" (5.1 cm) piece of 18-gauge wire. If necessary, use a metal file to smooth the ends. Use the tip of round-nose pliers to form a small P-shaped loop at one end (**a**).

Form a second, larger loop at the other wire end so the loops face in the same direction (**b**).

Use the largest portion of round-nose pliers to form a curve about three-quarters of the way down the wire from the large loop (**c**).

Use a jeweler's hammer and steel block to lightly tap the entire wire to harden the clasp.

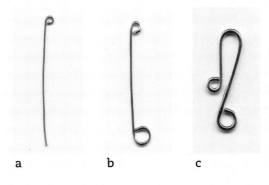

a   b   c

Two Dancers in Blue Earrings

Two Dancers in Blue

Edgar Degas (1834–1917) was born in Paris and studied at the École des Beaux-Arts. He then moved to Italy where he was influenced by the art of the Renaissance painters. Upon his return to Paris, he associated with the Impressionists and worked in painting, sculpture, printmaking, and drawing. Dancers were the subjects of more than half of his work. He is also known for his depictions of female nudes and horses. *Two Dancers in Blue* was painted in 1898 and is in the collection of the Louvre in Paris.

(Réunion des Musées Nationaux / Art Resource, NY)

LAYERS OF SIMPLE NETTING combine with crystals to form these fanciful earrings that mimic the tutus of Degas's ballerinas. The sky blue beads have an AB (aurora borealis) finish, which provides a depth of color to reflect the typical Impressionist style of painting—apply many colors and let the eyes make the mix.

FINISHED LENGTH:

2" (5 cm) long (including ear wire)
x 1 ³/₈" (3.5 cm) wide

TECHNIQUES:

netting, simple loops

MATERIALS AND TOOLS

· size 11° cylinder beads:
  10 g sky blue AB, 1 g silver-lined
  pale pink opal, 1 g silver lined
  jonquil opal

· 4mm faceted round crystal beads:
  pale topaz (4), light aqua (2)

· 6mm faceted round crystal
  beads (2), light aqua

· 22-gauge gold headpins (2),
  2" (5 cm)

· French ear wires (2), gold colored

· size D nylon beading thread

· wax or thread conditioner

· size 12 beading needle

· scissors

· wire cutters

· round-nose pliers

· flat-nose pliers

MAKING THE BEADED LAYERS

1 Thread a needle with 3' (1 m) of thread and wax well. Leaving a 4" (10 cm) tail, pick up twelve blue and one pink ("tip") cylinder beads. Pass back through the last blue bead added **(figure 1)**.

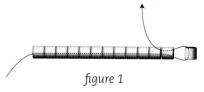

figure 1

2 Pick up eight blue beads, pass back through the third bead strung in the previous step, pick up one blue bead, and pass back through the first bead strung in the previous step **(figure 2)**.

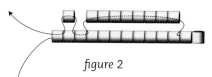

figure 2

3 Tie the working thread to the tail with a square knot.

4 Pick up one blue bead and pass through the first "up" bead from the previous row. Pick up ten blue beads and one jonquil ("tip") bead and pass back through the last blue bead added **(figure 3)**.

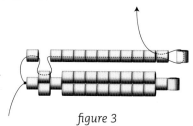

figure 3

5 Pick up eight blue beads and pass back through the second of the ten beads added in the previous step. Pick up one blue bead and pass back through the first bead added in the previous step **(figure 4)**.

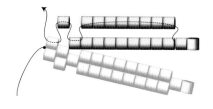

figure 4

6 Repeat steps 2, 4, and 5, alternating the color of the tip bead at each point, until you have fifteen points.

7 Make one more point, but instead of picking up a bead at the end, pass back through the "up" bead from the first set, joining the work into a circle (**figure 5**).

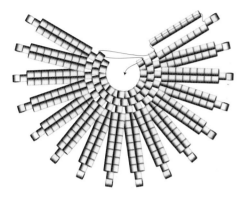

figure 5

8 Gather the beads along the inner edge of the circle, much like you'd gather fabric, by passing through an edge bead, skipping a bead, passing through the next edge bead in the opposite direction, skipping a bead, etc. Pull the thread taut, secure, and trim (**figure 6**).

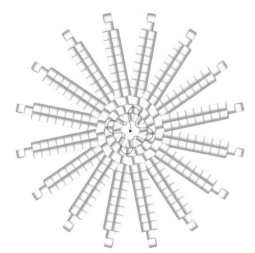

figure 6

9 Repeat steps 1 through 8 to make two more beaded layers, but make one by stringing ten beads in step 1 and six beads in step 4, and make the other by stringing eight beads in step 1 and four beads in step 4.

ASSEMBLING THE DANGLE

10 Onto the headpin string one 4mm topaz bead, one 6mm aqua bead, the small, medium, and large beaded layers, one 6mm aqua bead, one 4mm aqua bead, and one 4mm topaz bead (**figure 7**).

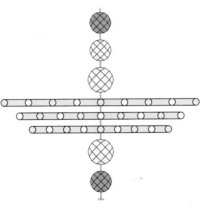

figure 7

11 With your fingers, bend the headpin over the top of the last bead forming a 90° angle (**figure 8**). Form a simple loop to secure the beads.

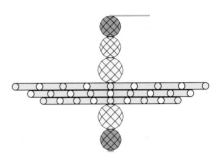

figure 8

12 Open the loop on the ear wire and slide the dangle onto the loop. Close the loop.

13 Repeat steps 1 through 13 to make the second earring.

The Lemon Ensemble

THIS SIMPLE PRINCESS-LENGTH necklace and accompanying earrings are easy to make, although their individual elements are certainly not plain. Like most Impressionist works of art, the beauty here is found in color, texture, shape, and placement. This design includes a nod to Manet's painting—the Venetian glass "lemon" is cocked to one side, adding a contemporary touch and a bit of whimsy.

FINISHED LENGTH:

18¼" (46.5 cm)

TECHNIQUES:

stringing, crimping, wrapped loop

MATERIALS AND TOOLS

- size 11° Japanese seed beads (29), matte olive
- 6mm round crystal pearls (6), bright gold
- 6mm round crystal pearls (5), dark green
- 9mm pressed glass spacers (6), gunmetal
- 14mm semiprecious blue tiger's eye flat twisted coin beads (24)
- 20 x 38mm blown Venetian glass dimpled oval bead (1), yellow and gold
- 6 x 8mm decorative oval jump ring (1), shiny brass
- 18mm magnetic hook clasp, shiny brass
- gold-filled crimp tubes (2)
- 22-gauge gold-filled head pins (2)
- gold-filled ear wires (2)
- medium-width flexible gold beading wire, 20" (60 cm)
- wire cutters
- crimping pliers
- chain-nose pliers
- round-nose pliers

MAKING THE NECKLACE

1 String one crimp tube and the clasp on the wire. Pass back through the crimp tube. Leaving a 1" (2.5 cm) tail, crimp the tube.

2 String a sequence of one coin and one seed bead ten times. String one gold pearl, one spacer, the Venetian bead, one spacer, one gold pearl, one coin, one green pearl, one coin, one green pearl, one seed bead, one coin, one seed bead, one green pearl, two seed beads, one coin, one seed bead, one green pearl, three seed beads, one coin, one green pearl, and four seed beads. String a sequence of one coin and one seed bead six times.

3 String one coin, one crimp tube, and the jump ring. Pass back through the crimp tube. Snug the beads and crimp. Trim any excess wire.

MAKING THE EARRINGS

1 Use a head pin to string one gold pearl, one spacer, one coin, one spacer, and one gold pearl.

2 Form a wrapped loop that attaches to an ear wire (**figure 1**).

figure 1

3 Repeat steps 1 and 2 to make a second earring.

The Perfect Crimp

When you attach the clasp and pass back through the crimp bead, leave at least ³/₈" (1 cm) of wire. Also, make sure the wires run along opposite sides of the crimp bead so the crimping action will separate the two. Keep rounding a crimped bead with the front notch on your crimping pliers. The metal is fairly malleable and can be shaped into a perfect cylinder.

DESIGNING STRUNG NECKLACES

The necklace in *The Lemon Ensemble* is a straight-forward design. You string beads onto a single flexible beading wire and add a clasp half at each end. This simple style can be a springboard for a wide variety of other necklace styles, too.

First, think about length. The necklace shown on page 30 is about 18" (45.7 cm), and hangs just below the collarbone. But you can make a necklace as short as a "dog collar" that fits snugly around the throat or as long as the flapper style that hangs mid-belly—or any length in between.

Next, think about bead placement. Do you want to string your beads in a repetitive pattern, or would an asymmetrical design work better? Maybe your beads would look best in a multi-strand design?

Consider choosing materials other than beads to string, such as dangles, charms, and pendants. You can make bead dangles by stringing beads onto a head pin and forming a wrapped loop to secure them. String the dangle onto the stringing wire as you would any bead.

Finally, remember that your findings are as much part of the overall design aesthetic as the beads themselves. There are innumerable variations in clasp, chain, head pin, crimp bead, jump ring, and connector styles, so keep your eyes open for styles you like.

Pollard Willows and
Setting Sun Brooch

Pollard Willows and Setting Sun

Vincent van Gogh (1853–1890) was born in Groot-Zundert, Holland, and led a short and tragic life. Plagued by low self-esteem and an overzealous religious passion, his early paintings were dark and haunting. With the help of his brother, Théo, he studied art in Paris where he met Paul Gauguin, Henri de Toulouse-Lautrec, and Georges Seurat. After moving to Arles in southern France, van Gogh lightened his palette with the colors of the Provençal landscape and painted his best works. Struggling with madness, van Gogh took his own life in 1890, having sold only one painting. *Pollard Willows and Setting Sun* was painted in 1888 and is housed at Rijksmuseum Kroeller-Mueller, Otterlo, The Netherlands.

(ART RESOURCE, NY)

THE INTENSE AND BRIGHT colors of van Gogh's painting are well represented in this golden agate donut. The stone has several shades of yellow, orange, red, and gray-green in subtle striations that mimic the artist's brush strokes. The crystal dangles were designed to resemble the artist's willow branches.

FINISHED LENGTH:

2" (5 cm) diameter

TECHNIQUES:

stringing

MATERIALS AND TOOLS

· 50mm golden agate donut (1)

· size 11° seed beads, 1 g light topaz

· size 15° seed beads, 1 g light topaz

· 4mm faceted round crystal:
  pale topaz (9), light aqua (9)

· 6mm fire-polished bicones,
  topaz (9)

· 6mm faceted round crystals,
  light aqua (9)

· 1" (2.5 cm) pin back (1)

· 6-lb. test braided beading thread

· size 12 beading needle

· scissors

· industrial-strength clear glue

MAKING THE CENTER DANGLE

1 Thread a needle with 3' (1 m) of thread. Pick up twenty-eight 11° beads or the number you need to make a loop around the donut. Pass back through the first bead strung and tie the working thread to the tail with a square knot **(figure 1)**.

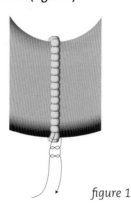

figure 1

2 Pick up fifteen 15° beads, one 4mm topaz crystal, one 4mm aqua crystal, one bicone, one 6mm crystal and one 15° bead. Skipping the 15° bead, pass back through all other beads strung in this step **(figure 2)**.

figure 2

3 Pass through all the beads strung in step 1, ending with the thread exiting the first bead strung (next to the knot) **(figure 3)**.

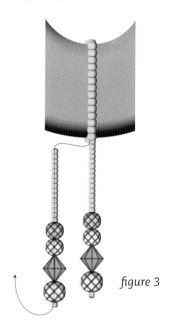

figure 3

4 Repeat steps 2 and 3 for the second dangle.

5 For the third strand, repeat steps 2 and 3 but begin with twenty 15° beads instead of fifteen.

6 Secure all threads and trim.

MAKING THE SIDE DANGLES

7 Working on one side of the center dangle, repeat steps 1 through 6 but make two strands with five 15° beads and one strand with ten 15° beads.

8 Repeat step 7 on other side of center dangle.

ATTACHING THE PIN BACK

9 Place a dab of glue on the pin back and attach it to the center top half of the back of the donut **(figure 4)**.

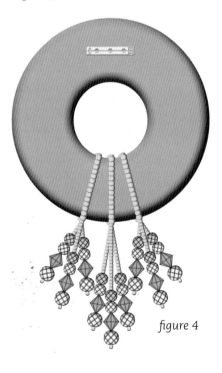

figure 4

ONE-OF-A-KIND GEMSTONES

Gemstones come in many different colors, from the bright blue of sapphire to the deep red of garnet and the lustrous green of jade. The range of color and patterning possible within one type of stone is quite vast.

Pollard Willows and Setting Sun Brooch features a donut of golden agate. If you were to order a stone like this from a catalog or online source, you may not get one that looks exactly like the one shown here. Golden agate can range from milky white to custard yellow to butterscotch, with bits of green, brown, and gray. The stone may have an orderly striation or be randomly spotted like this one. If you want to use a stone to simulate a specific color or design, it's best to select one up close and personal.

The Street Lamp Framed

The Street Lamp

Cornelio Geranzani (1880–1955) was born in Genoa, Italy. He wasn't an Impressionist painter per se, but he worked in the Italian Divisionism style, which was influenced by the Impressionist style, employing dots and strokes of pure colors. Geranzani interrupted his study of law to devote himself to painting full time. Retrospectives of his work have included as many as seventy-four catalogued paintings. *The Street Lamp* is in a private collection.

(ALINARI / ART RESOURCE, NY)

THE STREET LAMP FRAMED borrows the Impressionist technique of combining small amounts of different colors and letting the viewer's eyes do the mixing. Loomwork is a great technique for pictorial beadwork. The woven piece could also be appliquéd to a pillow or made into a focal piece on a purse or garment.

FINISHED LENGTH:

4³/₈" x 4⁷/₁₆" (11 x 11.5 cm)

TECHNIQUES:

loomwork

MATERIALS AND TOOLS

· size 11° cylinder beads:
   12 g opaque black
   1 g transparent orange AB
   1 g light daffodil
   2 g blue lined aqua
   1 g transparent light topaz
   5 g transparent dark sapphire
   5 g transparent dark topaz
   2 g transparent root beer
   10 g opaque royal blue
   2 g transparent emerald
   2 g transparent salmon
   1 g squash
   2 g transparent dark aqua
   1 g opaque bright red
   2 g transparent dark amethyst
   8 g opaque maroon
   5 g transparent rust

· size D nylon thread

· size 12 beading needle

· wax or thread conditioner

· scissors

· piece of cotton fabric,
  6" x 6" (15 x 15 cm)

· mat board, 8" x 10" (20.5 x 25.5 cm)

1 Prepare the bead mixes according to the chart on page 43. Keep them in small piles with a label indicating the mix letter.

2 Thread the loom with seventy-seven warp threads (the pattern is seventy-six beads wide).

3 Thread a needle with 3' (1 m) of thread and wax well. Leaving a 4" (10 cm) tail, tie the thread about 4" (10 cm) from the bottom of the leftmost warp thread .

4 Following the chart on page 42, weave seventy rows.

5 Cut the weaving from the loom. Weave in all ends and trim close.

6 Center the weaving on the fabric square **(figure 1)**.

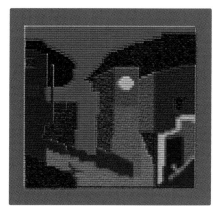

figure 1

7 Sew the weaving to the fabric, passing through edge beads and the fabric **(figure 2)**.

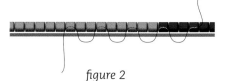

figure 2

8 Cut a center opening in the mat board according to the finished measurements of the beaded piece, in this case 4¹/₄" wide x 4¹/₂" tall (11 x 11.5 cm).

9 Use tape to mount the cloth to the back of the mat board, placing the weaving in the center opening. Place in a frame, if desired.

CHARTING ART *for* **LOOMWORK**

The chart presented for *The Street Lamp Framed* is on a square grid, but it didn't start that way. To get an accurate representation of a drawing when translating it into beadwork, you need to consider the shape of the beads. For loomwork done with 11° cylinder beads, you'll need graph paper that is 18 squares wide and 15 squares tall per inch (2.5 cm). You can find proportioned graph paper in some beading books or online.

1. Make a sketch or copy of the illustration you want to bead. If necessary, use a copy machine to resize the sketch to the desired finished size of the beadwork. *The Street Lamp Framed* is 4¼" wide x 4½" tall (11 x 11.5 cm).

2. Lay the proportioned graph paper over the illustration and hold the sheets against a sunny window or place on a light box. Trace the image onto the graph paper. *The Street Lamp Framed* worked out to be 76 beads wide by 70 beads tall.

3. You may finalize the graph on this paper or use the proportioned grid as a guide to outline the image square by square onto any size graph paper by hand or with a computerized drawing program. Then assign the colors.

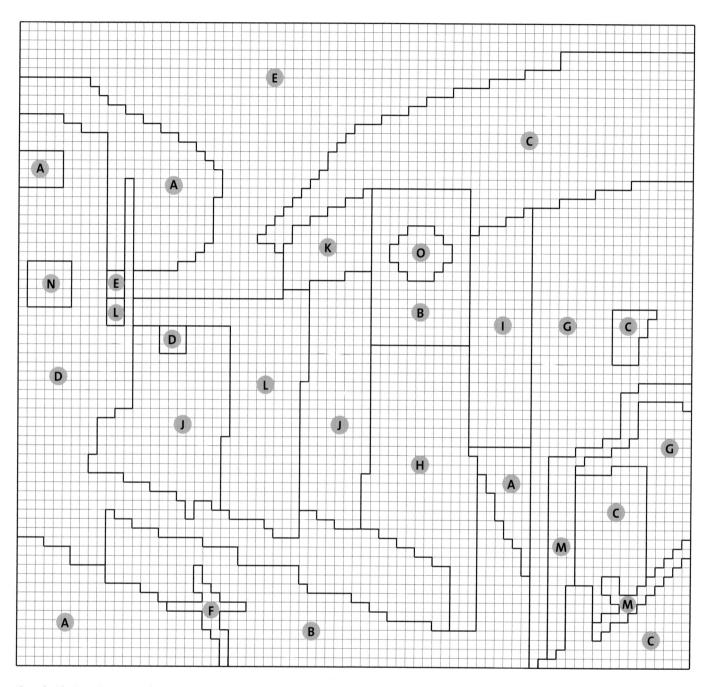

Chart for *The Street Lamp Framed*
(See facing page for description of bead colors.)

LETTER	BEAD COLORS	PROPORTIONS
A	black / maroon	(80% / 20%)
B	rust / dark topaz / amethyst / salmon	(equal parts)
C	black / royal blue	(80% / 20%)
D	maroon / black	(80% / 20%)
E	royal blue	
F	black	
G	sapphire / salmon	(equal parts)
H	rust / orange / emerald	(equal parts)
I	rust / salmon / dark topaz	(equal parts)
J	sapphire / light topaz / rust / dark topaz	(equal parts)
K	sapphire / rust / dark topaz / root beer	(equal parts)
L	blue-lined aqua / root beer	(equal parts)
M	squash / daffodil	(equal parts)
N	bright red	
O	daffodil	

Mango Woman Pendant

Woman with a Mango

Paul Gauguin (1848–1903) was born in France, moved to Peru as a toddler, and then back to France by age seven. He later became a stockbroker in Copenhagen where he lived with his Dutch wife and five children. Gauguin always had a passion for painting and collecting art and eventually left his family to pursue this passion full-time. He was an integral part of the Impressionist movement, but became deeply influenced by folk art and Japanese prints. The majority of Gauguin's work is considered Post-Impressionist, with its thematic imagery and bold planes of color. He spent much of his later life in French Polynesia, the subject of many of his paintings.

(ERIC LESSING / ART RESOURCE, NY)

THE SWIRLING, VOLUMINOUS fabric illustrated in Paul Gauguin's painting inspired the design of this spiraling pendant. Explore your local bead shop to find just the right colors of seed beads and drop beads to represent the dress. Allow your heart to flutter when you come across the perfect "mango" bead.

FINISHED LENGTH:

2" (5 cm) pendant

TECHNIQUES:

tubular peyote stitch, simple loop, crimping

MATERIALS AND TOOLS

· size 11° seed beads, 2 g each white-lined clear (A) and cornflower matte (B)

· size 8° seed beads, 2 g denim matte (C)

· 3mm fringe drops (23), sapphire matte AB (D)

· 4mm glass rounds (21), royal blue (E)

· 6 x 10mm fire-polished drops (2), orange

· 4 x 8mm vermeil Bali-style spacers (2)

· 3mm gold-filled crimp tubes (2)

· 22-gauge gold-filled head pins (2), 2" (5 cm)

· 22-gauge gold-filled eye pin (1), 2½" (6.5cm)

· vermeil hook and eye clasp with extender chain (1)

· 6-lb. test braided beading thread

· medium 24K gold flexible beading wire, 4 yd. (3.5 m)

· size 12 beading needle

· scissors

· wire cutters

· chain-nose pliers

· round-nose pliers

· crimping pliers

· bead clip

1 Thread the needle with 3' (1 m) of thread. Leaving a 4" (10 cm) tail, work rounds of tubular peyote stitch as follows:

ROUNDS 1 AND 2: Pick up two A, one E, two D, two C, and two B. Tie the beads into a circle. Pass through the beads to exit from the first A strung.

ROUND 3: Pick up one A and pass through the E of initial circle. Pull tight. Pick up one E, skip the next bead of the circle and pass through the next D. Pick up one D and pass through the next bead of the circle. Repeat around, skipping a bead and adding the same type you just exited. Keep a tight thread tension. Step up to the next round by stringing the last bead in the sequence and passing through the first A added in this round. This starts the spiral **(figure 1)**.

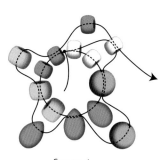

figure 1

ROUNDS 4 TO 7: Repeat round 3 for four rounds, working spiraling tubular peyote stitch. Always add the same type of bead you just exited.

ROUND 8: Work around the spiral. When you are ready to add B, pick up two B to make an increase and pass through the next A **(figure 2)**.

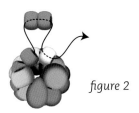

figure 2

ROUND 9: Work around the spiral. Work one B between the two added in round 7 to complete the increase and work one B to begin round 10 **(figure 3)**.

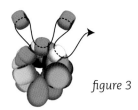

figure 3

ROUNDS 10 TO 13: Work around the spiral with no increases.

ROUNDS 14 AND 15: Repeat rounds 8 and 9, making the increase in the A position.

ROUNDS 16 TO 21: Work around the spiral with no increases. Weave through the beads as necessary to reinforce. Secure the thread and trim. Set the spiral aside.

2 String one fire-polished drop on a head pin. Form a simple loop to secure. Set aside. Repeat for the remaining fire-polished drop.

3 String one spacer, the spiral from the smallest point to the largest, and one spacer onto the eye pin. Form a simple loop to secure the beads. Attach one of the fire-polished bead dangles to the thin end of the pendant. Set aside **(figure 4)**.

figure 4

4 Cut the wire into seven 20" (51 cm) lengths.

5 Gather the wires together and trim as necessary to even out the ends. Pass one end of the gathered bunch through one crimp tube and one half of the clasp. Pass back through the crimp tube, leaving a 1" (2.5 cm) tail, and crimp. Trim any excess wire close to the crimp.

If all the wires won't fit when passing back through the tube, slide most of them through, crimp, and trim any excess wire above and below the crimp **(figures 5 and 6)**.

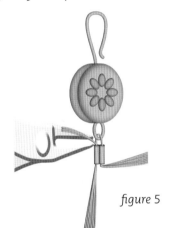

figure 5

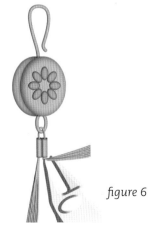

figure 6

6 With the wire ends still gathered, string the remaining crimp tubes. Place a bead clip on the wire ends so the wires stay even.

7 Slide the first tube just strung so it sits 1½" (4 cm) down from the first crimp. Crimp the tube. Repeat, crimping the remaining tubes onto the wire at 1½" (4 cm) intervals. Remove the bead clip.

8 Slide the pendant on the wires.

9 Repeat step 5 to attach the other half of the clasp.

10 Connect the remaining fire-polished drop dangle to the end of the extender chain.

Le Cirque Bracelet

Le Cirque

Georges Seurat (1859–1891) was
born in Paris to a wealthy family
and attended the prestigious École
des Beaux-Arts. Seurat was like a
scientist in his study of color and
how the eye perceives it. He was one
of the founders of the Neo-Impres-
sionist movement, and his technique
for creating shapes with pixel-like
characteristics came to be known as
Pointillism. Seurat kept his personal
life very secret, and even his closest
friends didn't find out until after
his death at age thirty-one that he
had a mistress and child. Although
unfinished, *Le Cirque* was his last
large-scale painting.

(*Erich Lessing / Art Resource, NY*)

THE DESIGN OF THIS JANGLY, colorful bracelet evokes the
flurry of activity in Georges Seurat's painting. Circular
peyote-stitched charms represent the circus ring, and
flame-like netted shapes signify the horse, clowns, and
ringmaster. The bracelet is surprisingly easy to make
and, once finished, a real attention-getter.

FINISHED LENGTH:

7½" (19 cm)

TECHNIQUES:

circular peyote stitch, netting, wrapped loop

MATERIALS AND TOOLS

· size 14°, 11°, and 8° Czech seed beads, 50 g in an assortment of reds, oranges, yellows, blues, and whites

· 3mm Japanese fringe drops, 3 g burgundy

· 4mm drops, 2 g light gold

· 14mm pressed-glass flat rounds with swirls (7), yellow AB

· 4mm crystal bicones (30) in an assortment of opaque white, topaz, and dark red

· 6mm crystal rounds (2), sapphire and topaz

· 8mm crystal rounds (10), in an assortment of topaz and dark red

· 22-gauge sterling silver head pins (24), 2" (5 cm)

· 5mm sterling silver jump rings (38)

· 12mm sterling silver charm bracelet with connector links and clasp, 7½" (19 cm)

· 6-lb. test braided beading thread, black

· size 10 and 12 beading needles

· scissors

· wire cutters

· round-nose pliers

· chain-nose pliers

MAKING THE CIRCLES

1 Thread the needle with 3' (1 m) of thread. Leaving a 4" (10 cm) tail, pick up six 11° beads and tie a knot to form a circle. Pass through the first bead strung.

2 Pick up one 14° bead and pass through the next bead of the initial circle. Repeat around to add six beads in all. Weave through the beads to exit from the first bead added in this round (**figure 1**).

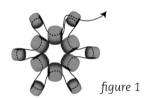

figure 1

3 Pick up three 11° beads and pass through the next bead added in the previous round. Repeat around to add eighteen beads in all. Weave through the beads to exit from the second bead added in this round (**figure 2**).

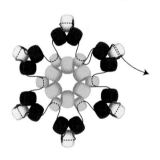

figure 2

4 Pick up three 11° beads and pass through the second bead of the next three-bead set in the previous round. Repeat around to add eighteen beads in all. Weave through the beads to exit from the second bead added in this round (**figure 3**).

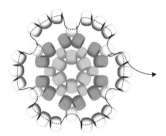

figure 3

5 *Pick up one 11° bead, skip one bead, and pass through the next bead added in the previous round. Pick up one 11° bead and pass through the first bead of the next three-bead set from the previous round. Repeat from * around to add twelve beads in all. Weave through the beads to exit from the first bead added in this round (**figure 4**).

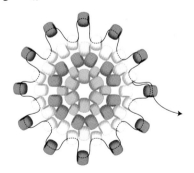

figure 4

6 Pick up six 14° beads and pass through the bead just exited to make a loop. Weave through these beads twice more to reinforce. Secure the thread and trim.

7 Repeat steps 1 through 6 to make nineteen circle charms of varied colors. The circle described makes a very flat, even charm, but the charms shouldn't all be perfectly constructed. Strive for a freeform look by altering the bead number per stitch or per round, changing bead sizes in each round, or adding rounds. Set aside.

MAKING THE DIAMONDS

8 Thread the needle with 3' (1 m) of thread. Leaving a 4" (10 cm) tail, pick up six 14° beads and tie a knot to form a circle. Pick up sixteen 11° beads and one drop. Pass back through the last 11° bead strung. Pick up three 11° beads, skip two beads on the initial strand, and pass through the next bead. Repeat across the strand to make five nets. Weave through the initial loop to turn the needle around and pass back through the last two beads added in this row **(figure 5)**.

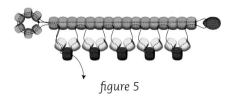

figure 5

9 Pick up three 11° beads and pass through the second bead of the next net. Repeat across the row, making four nets in all. Pick up one 14° bead and pass back through the last two beads added in this row **(figure 6)**.

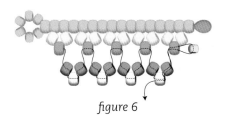

figure 6

10 Make two more decreasing rows of nets, using a 14° bead to make the turnaround as before. When there are just two nets left, connect the midpoints with a crystal, drop, or other accent bead.

11 Weave to the initial strand and work a series of nets to mirror the first, creating a diamond shape.

12 Repeat steps 8 through 11 to make nineteen diamonds of varied colors. As with the circle charms, go for a freeform look by changing the bead number per stitch or by throwing in different bead sizes at random. Set aside.

MAKING THE DANGLES

13 String one 14mm bead on a head pin and form a wrapped loop that attaches to a link on the charm bracelet **(figure 7)**.

figure 7

Repeat to add the remaining 14mm beads along the length of the bracelet. Do the same with the 8mm crystals. Balance the placement so there are dangles along each edge of the bracelet, not just one side.

14 Slide a ½" (1.5 cm) assortment of crystals and seed beads on a head pin and form a wrapped loop that attaches to one of the links. Repeat to add varied dangles down each edge of the bracelet.

15 Use jump rings to attach the circle and diamond charms to the bracelet.

The Banana Plantation Necklace

Banana Plantation

Pierre Auguste Renoir was born in Limoges, France, in 1841. He was introduced to the art world while he was working in a factory, painting designs on the famous porcelain named for his hometown. Renoir is one of the best-known artists of all time and is closely associated with the Impressionist movement. He painted *Banana Plantation* in 1881.

(ERICH LESSING / ART RESOURCE, NY)

THIS COLORFUL PAINTING by Pierre Auguste Renoir is full of texture and natural forms, which inspired the colors and elements of this necklace. The multicolored branch fringe mimics the seemingly random direction of the leaves. The focal bead echoes the sole tree in the background. The centerpiece is suspended from lengths of tubular herringbone stitch that are joined with a button-and-loop closure.

FINISHED LENGTH:

21" (53 cm)

TECHNIQUES:

tubular herringbone stitch, branch fringe, even-count peyote stitch

MATERIALS AND TOOLS

· size 11° seed beads: 12 g topaz, 12 g green, 12 g pale yellow AB, 3 g teal AB, 1 g blue

· 6mm fire-polished glass beads (5), topaz

· 10mm spacers (8), antiqued gold-tone

· focal bead (1)

· ½" (1.5 cm) button (1)

· size D nylon beading thread in color to match beads

· beeswax or synthetic wax

· size 12 beading needle

· scissors

1 Pour all of the 11° seed beads into one container and shake them around to create a "bead soup." While working with the soup, try not to pay too much attention the order in which you pick up the beads—the mix should be random.

2 Thread a needle with approximately 3' (1 m) of thread and wax well. Leaving a 10" (25.5 cm) tail, which you'll use for the closure, work six-bead tubular herringbone stitch with the seed bead mix until the piece measures 6¾" (17 cm).

3 Decrease three beads by working one round, picking up only one bead instead of two in each stitch **(figure 1)**.

figure 1

4 Exiting the first bead in this last round, pick up one spacer, one fire-polished bead, one spacer, and one seed bead. Pass back down through the spacer, fire-polished bead, and spacer, then pass through the same seed bead you began with **(figure 2)**.

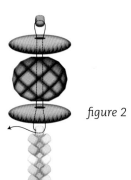

figure 2

*Pass through the next seed bead in the round and then pass through the spacer, fire-polished bead, and spacer previously strung. Pick up one seed bead and pass back down through the spacer, fire-polished bead, and spacer, then pass through the same seed bead you began with. Repeat from * one more time. You now have a tube, a spacer, a fire-polished bead, a spacer, and a cluster of three seed beads **(figure 3)**.

figure 3

5 Pass through the spacer, fire-polished bead, spacer, and one of the seed beads added in step 4. Pick up one seed bead, pass through the next seed bead added in step 4, pick up one seed bead, pass through the next seed bead added in step 4, pick up one seed bead and pass through the last of the three seed beads added in step 4. You now have a ring of six seed beads **(figure 4)**.

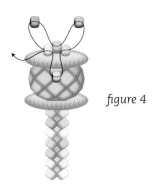

figure 4

6 Work tubular herringbone stitch until the new section measures 5" (12.5 cm). Repeat steps 3 through 5. Work a third section of tubular herringbone stitch that measures 6¾" (17 cm).

7 Repeat steps 3 and 4. Exiting from one of the three seed beads just added, pick up eight to ten seed beads. Slide the button's shank over these beads and pass back through the same bead you began with. Pass through the next seed bead added in step 5, then pass through the seed bead loop again. Repeat this two or three more times to secure the button end of the closure **(figure 5)**.

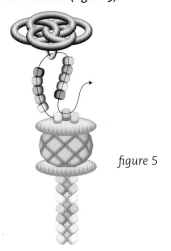

figure 5

8 Using the beginning tail, repeat steps 3 and 4. Working as you did for the button end, add a loop of seed beads long enough to slide snugly over the button. Reinforce the loop by passing through it several times. Secure the thread and trim. Set the necklace aside **(figure 6)**.

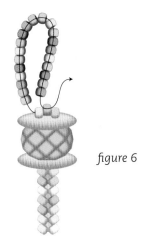

figure 6

9 Thread a needle with approximately 3' (1 m) of thread and wax well. Leaving a 6" (15 cm) tail, pick up one spacer, one fire-polished bead, one spacer, the focal bead, and one spacer. *Use seed beads to make one strand of branch fringe ten beads long. Pass back up through the spacer, focal bead, spacer, fire-polished bead, and spacer (the "pendant beads"). Pick up one seed bead and pass down through the pendant beads. Repeat from * one more time. You now have two seed beads at the top of the pendant beads. Add several more strands of branch fringe of slightly varying lengths, passing through the pendant beads and one of the two top seed beads each time.

10 Create a hanging bail of peyote stitch two beads wide at the top of the pendant. Exiting from left to right out of the right-side seed bead, pick up one seed bead and pass through the left seed bead. Pick up one seed bead and pass back through the bead just added. Repeat until the strip measures approximately 1½" (4 cm) or is long enough to comfortably fit around the herringbone tube **(figure 7)**.

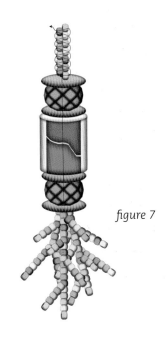

figure 7

The Bail

To ensure that the bail will move freely when the branch fringe is completed, check the bail's movement after each addition you make close to it. If you've inadvertently passed through a bead in the bail, you can easily fix the problem by removing the offending strand of fringe.

11 Loop the strip over the center tubular herringbone-stitched section and sew the last row to the first row. Pass through the beads several times to secure **(figure 8)**.

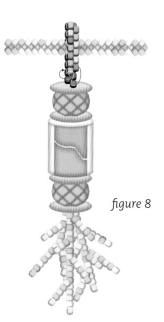

figure 8

12 Start a new thread that exits from a seed bead at one end of the center tubular herringbone-stitched section. Work strands of branch fringe that are each ½" to ¾" (1.5 to 2 cm) long into the beads of the tube. The fringe should be dense, worked into almost every bead of the tube.

When you reach the center, slide the bail onto the tube. Pass through two beads under the bail and continue with branch fringe on the other side of the bail until the rest of the center tube is covered. Secure the thread and trim. The bail should move freely over the tube so that it hangs correctly each time you put the necklace on **(figure 9)**.

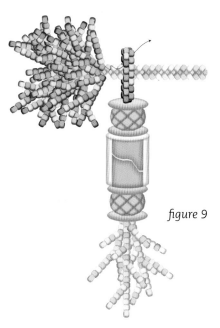

figure 9

THE FRINGE ELEMENT

The Banana Plantation Necklace uses branch fringe on the centerpiece to mimic the branches and leaves on the banana trees in the painting. Here are three other fringing techniques you can use to embellish your beadwork. Fringes can also be added to the edges of fabric.

1. Simple Fringe. Anchor your thread in the beadwork or fabric to be fringed. String beads to the desired length. Skip the last bead strung, pass back through all the beads in the strand, pass back into the beadwork or fabric. Strands can all be the same length or varied lengths. For thick fringe, add more than one strand at the same place.

2. Looped Fringe. Anchor your thread in the beadwork or fabric to be fringed. String enough beads to make a loop the desired length. Pass back into the beadwork or fabric one or two bead widths from where you began. Continue making loops, passing through the previous loop to intertwine the loops if desired.

3. Netted Fringe. Anchor your thread in the beadwork or fabric to be fringed. Work netting as desired, passing back through the beadwork or fabric at the proper distance to keep the netting from kinking.

simple fringe

looped fringe

netted fringe

Morning on the Seine Bracelet

Morning on the Seine near Giverny

Claude Monet (1840–1926) was born in Paris but spent his youth in Le Havre, France. Upon his return to Paris, he associated with the artists Renoir, Pissarro, and Sisley, and exhibited his works alongside theirs in the first exhibition of Impressionist work in 1874. Monet is recognized as one of the creators of Impressionism, and he was one of its most consistent exponents. *Morning on the Seine near Giverny* was painted in 1897.

(ART RESOURCE, NY)

CLAUDE MONET'S INTERPRETATION of the morning fog and clouds reflected in the waters of the Seine River evokes an ethereal quality. This airiness and weightlessness is likewise expressed in the bracelet by the rings that encircle the blue stones and include small silver-lined seed beads that seem to float above the cloudlike drop beads.

FINISHED LENGTH:

7" (18 cm)

TECHNIQUES:

tubular peyote stitch, peyote-stitch decreases

MATERIALS AND TOOLS

· 35mm faceted stone slice bead (1), blue quartz

· 20mm faceted stone slice beads (2), blue chalcedony

· 3–4mm drops (114), matte crystal AB

· size 11° seed beads, 5 g pale blue

· size 11° hex beads (85), clear AB

· size 15° seed beads (119), silver-lined blue

· size 15° charlottes, 3 g matte crystal

· 6mm round crystal or fire-polished beads (2), light sapphire

· 6-lb. test braided beading thread

· size 12 beading needle

· scissors

BEZELING THE LARGE STONE

1 Thread a needle with approximately 5' (1.5 m) braided beading thread. Pick up an even number of 11° beads to encircle the 35mm stone—this stone required seventy-eight beads. Leaving an 8" (20.5 cm) tail, pass through all the beads again to form a circle **(figure 1)**.

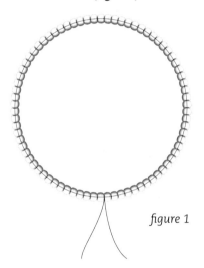

figure 1

2 Work three rounds of even-count tubular peyote stitch with 11° beads. Repeat two more times to make a band that is five rows deep **(figure 2)**.

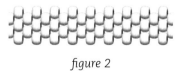

figure 2

3 Work one round of peyote stitch with hex beads, followed by two rounds of charlottes **(figure 3)**. Work with tight tension so the top rounds of charlottes pull in, forming a cup.

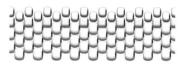

figure 3

4 Weave through the beads to exit from the opposite side of the bezel. Fit the stone into the bezel. Work one round of peyote stitch with hex beads, followed by two rounds of charlottes, again working with tight tension and pulling the beads in to form a cup. Work one round of charlottes, decreasing every third bead **(figure 4)**.

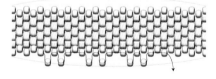

figure 4

5 Weave through the beads to exit from an 11° bead in the middle round. Pick up one drop bead and pass through the next 11° bead in the round. Repeat around the bezel, adding thirty-nine drop beads total **(figure 5)**.

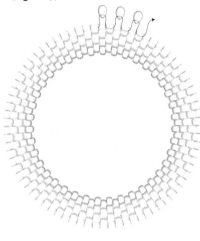

figure 5

6 Weave through the beads to exit from an 11° bead one round toward the front of the bezel. Pick up one charlotte, one 15° bead, one charlotte, and pass through the next 11° bead in the round. Pull the thread tight to make the beads click into place **(figure 6)**. Secure the thread and trim close to the beadwork.

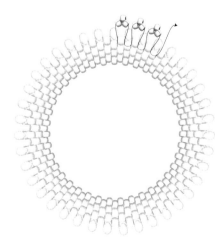

figure 6

BEZELING THE SMALL STONES

7 Follow the instructions for the large stone, beginning with a ring— this stone required forty-six beads. Add one decrease round of charlottes (step 4) on the front and the back, then one even row of charlottes, working one bead over the decrease points **(figure 7).** Embellish as for the large stone. Secure the thread and trim close to the beadwork.

Repeat for the remaining stone.

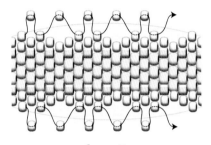

figure 7

JOINING THE BEZEL

8 Working with the larger bezel, weave the tail through the beads to exit from an 11° bead on the last round on the back. *Pick up an 11°, skip a bead, and pass through the next bead. Repeat from * three more times to create four "up" beads **(figure 8)**.

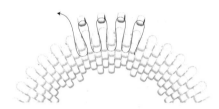

figure 8

9 Turn the work around. Use 11° beads to work five rows of peyote stitch off of the "up" beads added in the previous step. You now have a tab that is eight beads wide and six rows long **(figure 9)**.

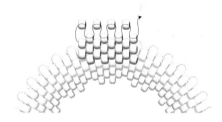

figure 9

10 Join this tab to the bottom row of 11° beads on the back of one of the smaller stones (**figure 10**).

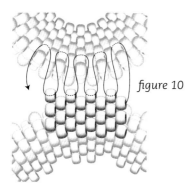

figure 10

11 Repeat steps 8 through 10 to join the second small bezel to the large bezel on the opposite side.

MAKING THE BAND

12 As with joining the bezels, start a strip of peyote stitch that is eight beads wide opposite the joining tab on one of the small bezels. Continue for twenty-eight rows or to desired length. Don't trim the thread. Repeat for the other end.

One-Loop Closure

For a one-loop closure, make one side of the clasp with a large button or bead. For the other side, make one large loop and span the entire width of the band, beginning with the outermost bead on one side and ending with the outermost bead on the other.

MAKING THE BEAD AND LOOP CLOSURE

13 With the thread exiting from an end bead in the last row and traveling toward the outer edge, pick up three 11° beads, one 6mm bead, one charlotte, one 15° bead, and one charlotte. Pass back through the 6mm bead and one 11° bead. Pick up two 11° beads and pass through the next "up" bead of the last row, traveling again toward the outer edge of the band. Weave through the band so you are exiting from the next "up" bead, traveling toward the center of the band. Repeat the stringing sequence above and pass through the last "up" bead, again traveling toward the center of the band. Reinforce the connection. Secure thread and trim close to beadwork (**figure 11**).

figure 11

14 For the loop end of the closure, work as for the bead end, but pick up nineteen 11° beads in place of the 6mm bead, charlotte, 15° bead, charlotte sequence (**figure 12**).

figure 12

EMBELLISHING THE BAND

15 With a new thread exiting from a corner band bead, pick up one 15° bead, one drop bead, and one 15° bead. Pass down through the next bead on the edge of the band and up through the following bead. *Pick up one drop and one 15° bead, pass down into the next bead on the edge of the band and up through the following bead. Repeat to the end of this edge, then repeat the entire process for the remaining three band edges. Secure all threads and trim close to the beadwork (**figure 13**).

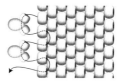

figure 13

BEADING BEZELS

The stone slices in *Morning on the Seine Bracelet* have bezels made with varying sizes of seed beads. The largest—11° seed beads—are in the rows that encircle the stone. As the bezel comes up over the front and back of the stone, progressively smaller beads are used—15° seed beads and charlottes. The smaller beads make the bezel circumference smaller, thereby securing the stone.

To make a bezel with all the same size beads, begin decreasing the number of beads in a round as you come up over the front and back of the stone. You'll have to experiment with the number of decreases to get the perfect fit, but begin by decreasing about 20 percent. For the large stone in this bracelet, it would work out to decreasing once every four or five beads.

If you have a flat-backed stone, you could use leather or a heavy fabric for the back of the bezel. Glue the stone to the leather or fabric. When the glue is dry, use backstitch to sew a circle of an even number of beads at the base of the stone. Use this base to proceed with one of the two methods described above. Carefully trim the leather or fabric close to the backstitched round.

Mardi Gras Bracelet

Mardi Gras

Paul Cézanne (1839–1906) was born in Aix-en-Provence in southern France, where he studied drawing and befriended the author Emile Zola. Much to the chagrin of his well-off banker father, Cézanne eventually joined Zola in Paris to become a painter. There he met Camille Pissarro and other members of the Impressionist movement. He was always the outsider, however, as he was drawn to still-life scenes and to more solid forms than his colleagues were. Although not recognized as a superstar during most of his lifetime, Cézanne greatly influenced later artists. Pablo Picasso said that Cézanne was "my one and only master . . . the father of us all."

(Scala / Art Resource, NY)

CARNIVAL IS AN ONGOING celebration when you wear this peyote- and brick-stitched bracelet. It incorporates the colors of Cézanne's subjects, Pierrot and Harlequin, but can also be made with any color combination. This version is made with dark thread and white beads to imitate Cézanne's extreme shadows.

FINISHED LENGTH:

7 ½" (19 cm)

TECHNIQUES:

flat peyote stitch, peyote-stitch increases and decreases, brick stitch, simple fringe, knotting

MATERIALS AND TOOLS

· size 11° Japanese seed beads,
  10 g shiny red (A)

· size 12° Czech true-cut seed beads,
  10 g shiny black (B)

· size 11° Japanese seed beads,
  10 g shiny white (C)

· size 15° Japanese seed beads,
  3 g transparent gold (D)

· 5mm vintage sequins (200),
  white AB

· 23mm vintage glass button
  with shank (1), black

· 8mm seamstress hook-and-loop
  closure (1), black

· 6-lb. test braided beading
  thread, black

· scissors

· size 11 beading needle

1 Thread the needle with 3' (1 m) of thread. Leaving a 4" (10 cm) tail, pick up one A, seventeen B, and two A. Skip the last two A and pass back through the last B strung. Work across the row in peyote stitch. String one A and tie a square knot to place the end A beads next to each other. Pass through one of these A beads to set up for the next row **(figure 1)**.

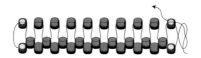

figure 1

2 Work one A in the next stitch. Work seven stitches using B. String one A and pass the needle between the beads of the previous rows, and pass back through the A to make the turnaround **(figure 2)**.

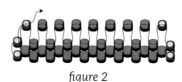

figure 2

3 Continue to work decreasing peyote stitch, adding one A at each end and B in the middle to make a half-diamond that's ten rows long. (The tenth row will be one A.) Maintain a very tight tension so the beadwork begins to cup.

4 Weave through the beads to exit from the A on the opposite side of the knot. Repeat steps 2 and 3 to create the other side of the diamond. Secure the thread and trim. Set aside.

5 Repeat steps 1 to 4 seven times to make eight diamonds in all.

6 Start a new thread that exits from the tenth-row bead of one of the diamonds. Pass down through the tenth-row bead of a second diamond, making sure the diamonds have the same side facing up. Pass up through the tenth-row bead of the first diamond so the two are connected **(figure 3)**.

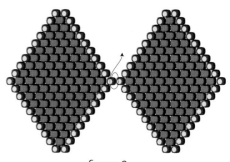

figure 3

7 Pass up through the adjacent ninth-row A. String one A, pass under the thread bridge between the beads connected in the last step and then back through the A to make a brick stitch. Pass down through the adjacent ninth-row A on the second diamond. Weave through the B on the second diamond to exit up through the eighth-row A as shown in the drawing **(figure 4)**.

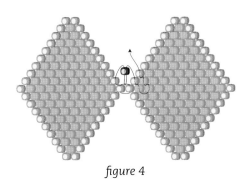

figure 4

8 Continue using A to work brick stitches between the diamonds. Add two A in the next row, three A in the following, and so on until you connect the first-row A beads of each diamond with nine stitches. The triangle created will buckle slightly, exaggerating the shape of the diamonds. Secure the thread and trim.

9 Repeat steps 6 to 8 to connect the diamonds to form a band.

10 Start a new thread that exits from the bottom A of a diamond at one end of the band. Pick up three C and pass under the thread bridge between the two A, and pass up through the third C just strung. *Pick up two C, pass under the thread bridge between the next two A and pass up through the second C just strung **(figure 5)**.

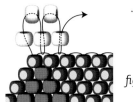

figure 5

Repeat from * around the entire band to create a simple three-bead edging. When you work the pointed ends of the band, make the passes under the threads that hold the rows together—there are no regular thread bridges.

11 Start a new thread that exits from the point at one end of the band. Use C to work four rows of three-bead-wide peyote stitch to make a small tab **(figure 6)**.

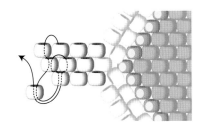

figure 6

12 Sew the button to the front side of the tab, weaving through it several times to reinforce. The button is only decorative, but should still be secured to the front of the bracelet. Stitch the loop half of the closure underneath the button on the back side of the tab. Pass through the beads and the loop several times to reinforce the connection. Secure the thread and trim.

13 Start a new thread that exits from the point at the opposite end of the band. Use C to work four rows of three-bead-wide peyote stitch to make a small tab. Sew the hook to the front of the tab so the hook points up toward the front of the bracelet. Pass through the beads and hook several times to reinforce the connection. Secure the thread and trim.

14 Exit from one of the "up" beads of the edging. Pick up two C and pass through the next up bead to make a peyote-stitched increase. Repeat around the entire bracelet. The edging will ruffle. Make a second row of peyote stitch, this time stringing one C, one sequin, and one D. Pass back through the sequin. Pass through the C just added and the next set of two C from the previous row **(figure 7)**.

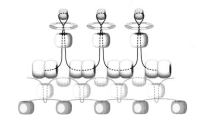

figure 7

15 Repeat around the bracelet. If necessary, add extra sequins to the area around the button and closure to hide the stitches there. Secure the thread and trim.

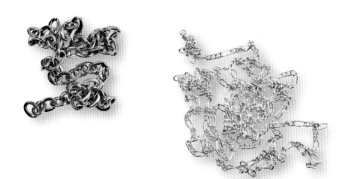

tools and techniques

stocking your stash

A beader's stash, or collection of beads and beading materials, often resembles a miniature bead shop. But a fully loaded beading arsenal isn't absolutely necessary to complete the projects in *Beadwork Inspired by Art: Impressionist Jewelry and Accessories*—you'll just need a few essentials. Use the materials and tools list at the beginning of each project as your shopping guide. Your bead stash will simply grow over time as you continue to make new projects.

Any bead stash, no matter how meager, contains a wide array of materials for creating beadwork. The many bits and pieces are too numerous to mention, so we've provided brief descriptions of the specific items you'll need for the projects in this book. If you're an established beader, you might have many of these things on hand, but it never hurts to have a little review to be sure you've covered the bases. If you're new to beading, read through these descriptions so you'll know exactly what to ask for as you get busy stocking your stash.

BEADS

What we're here for! The love of beading starts with beads, from the sparkling crystal to the humble seed.

BLOWN-GLASS BEADS are made in a furnace. Air is literally blown through the glass to create a bubble, making a surprisingly strong, but hollow bead. Venice is famous for its blown-glass beads, and they can be found in most high-end bead shops.

CRYSTAL BEADS are made of leaded glass—that is, glass that has been manufactured with lead oxide. The high lead content (up to 35 percent) causes the glass to refract light more than regular glass does. The most famous and sparkly crystals come from Austria, where top-secret machines cut the sharpest, most precise facets, adding to the dazzling light display. Beware of the holes in crystals because they are sharp and can easily cut thread. To prevent a potential beading disaster, add a seed bead to each side of the crystal to act as a buffer.

FIRE-POLISHED BEADS are made of leaded glass, too, but they don't have as high a lead content as the crystals described above. These beads are made in the Czech Republic, so they are sometimes called "Czech crystals." Although they aren't as sparkly as Austrian crystals, they are beautiful nonetheless—and a less expensive way to add shimmer to your beadwork.

PRESSED-GLASS BEADS are also produced in the Czech Republic. They are available in a staggering array of shapes, sizes, colors, and finishes. To make them, molten glass is poured into a mold. Typical pressed-glass beads include flowers and leaves, but also available are rounds, ovals, squares, pyramids, barrels, and other novelty shapes (such as cat faces and skulls).

LAMPWORKED BEADS are one of the oldest types of glass beads. They're made by heating a cane of glass over a torch and then winding the hot glass onto a metal wire. This is a relatively crude process for making beads, as the results aren't uniform, but this technique has had a huge renaissance in the last decade, and skilled artisans have brought the craft to a new artistic level. Also called "art beads," because they're individually made, lampworked beads are available in a variety of glass types and finishing techniques, which makes each bead unique.

METAL BEADS are made with all kinds of metals. The most common are sterling and fine silver, brass, gold filled, and vermeil (which is made by adding a 24-karat gold coating over a sterling silver base bead). Metal beads come in a wide array of shapes, so they make great accents when combined with more colorful beads. They also make a strong statement on their own.

PEARL BEADS are natural mollusk-produced beads. The most common types found in bead shops are the freshwater variety, most likely from China, although Japan and India produce them in large quantities, too. Pearl farmers insert either a shell or plastic base into a mollusk. The mollusk makes itself more comfortable by secreting a smooth coating, or nacre, over this base. Different mollusks produce different-colored pearls, but some pearls are dyed. If you buy dyed pearls, ask the salesperson if the color will rub off. If so, leave them at the store—or, when you get home, give them a light coat of clear acrylic spray paint. Pearls usually have small holes, so you'll need to use thin wire or stitch with a thin beading needle when working with them.

SEED BEADS are so named because of their diminutive size. They are made by first heating glass and pulling it into a long cane, then blowing a hole down the center of the cane. The cane is chopped into little pieces and heated or tumbled to soften the edges.

Seed beads come in all different sizes, from the size of a pomegranate seed to a celery seed. The size is indicated by an "aught," or °. The larger the bead, the smaller the aught number. The most common sizes are between 15° and 6°.

Seed beads come primarily from the Czech Republic and Japan. *Czech seed beads* have slightly smaller holes than the Japanese kind and are somewhat irregular in shape.

Japanese seed beads are very uniform and have a bit wider hole.

Cylinder beads are another type of Japanese seed bead. They are extremely uniform, have thin walls, and also have a very wide hole.

All seed beads come in a wide range of colors, finishes, and cuts. For example, a size 13° or 14° Czech seed bead with facets is called a *charlotte*. A size 12° Czech seed bead with one facet is called a *true cut*. A Japanese seed bead that has six sides is called a *hex*, and Japanese seed beads with three sides are called triangles.

There are other glass, seedlike beads out there, too, including drops and bugles. Although they aren't officially labeled as seed beads, they're made in much the same way. You'll find them in the seed-bead section of the bead store. *Drops*, sometimes called fringe beads or magatamas, look like size 6° seed beads with an off-center hole. These work great for embellishing fringe.

Bugles are about the same width as a size 10° seed bead, but are much longer and are often faceted. Beware— they have sharp edges. (As when working with crystals, a good habit to prevent a beading catastrophe is to use a seed bead at each end to act as a buffer.)

STONE BEADS are made out of just about any type of stone you can think of, including rubies and diamonds. They come from all over the world, and vary in price depending on the value of the stone.

Many stone beads are round, but you will also find rondelles, ovals, and other shapes, including donuts. Tumbled-stone nugget and chip beads are also very popular. When you buy stone beads, inquire about whether they've been dyed or not. A surface dye will eventually fade, so even though they might look pretty at the store, you might want to leave dyed beads out of your shopping tray.

SEQUINS, although frequently found in fabric shops, are beads, too! (Technically, anything with a hole through it qualifies as a bead.) Sequins are made of plastic and are available in every color imaginable. Beaders find endless ways to embellish their work with sequins, and the vintage varieties are especially sought after.

FINDINGS

Like a wooden truss, door handle, or the stained-glass windowpanes of a grand hotel or cathedral, findings are what support, open and close, and sometimes embellish your beaded jewelry.

BUTTONS are great for decorating pieces, but they can also function as closures for a loop/button clasp as for the *Mardi Gras Bracelet* on page 64.

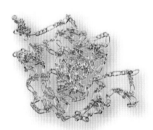

CHAIN serves as necklace straps, holds bead dangles together, or simply embellishes your jewelry. You'll be surprised by the wide variety of link shapes and sizes. You might want to consider using individual chain links as decorative jump rings—just use two pairs of chain-nose pliers to open each link (see page 88).

CLASPS are the closures you'll need to finish off a necklace, bracelet, or anklet. There are dozens of different types. In this book we've primarily used box clasps and hook-and-eye clasps.

Hook-and-eye clasps are shaped as their name describes and are closed by hooking into a jump ring or chain.

Box clasps have a springy metal tab on one side. The other side has a metal box into which you place the tab.

CRIMP BEADS and crimp tubes are tiny metal beads that secure flexible beading wire to findings. To avoid frustration, stick to buying sterling silver or gold-filled crimp beads or tubes—they work the best. See page 80 for instructions on how to crimp. Be sure to use crimping pliers (see page 79) to achieve the most professional-looking results.

EAR WIRES are used to attach earring dangles to pierced ears. The most common, French ear wires, are shaped like a **J,** but there are several other types to choose from, too.

EYE PINS are thin pieces of wire that have a loop at one end. They are often used to make bead links.

HEAD PINS consist of a thin wire with a flat, perpendicular disk at one end. In jewelry making, they're most often used to create dangles.

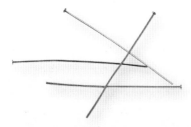

JUMP RINGS are so named because of their function— they act as a link, or "jump," from one section of a piece of jewelry to another. They are made up of circles or ovals of wire, often with a slit on one side that can be opened and closed with chain-nose pliers. See page 88 for the proper technique for opening and closing jump rings.

PIN BACKS are great when you want to turn a piece of beadwork into a brooch or pin. They usually have a flat metal portion onto which you sew the work and a levered pin on the back that's secured by a spring-loaded closure.

STRINGING MATERIALS

Just as an artist needs a canvas, you need a good strong base onto which to work your beaded art. Stringing materials are the backbone of a beaded piece, so don't skimp when it comes to quality. Although threads and wires might not be the most exciting part of the piece, they're holding it all together, so take care to get the best type.

NYLON BEADING THREAD is made up of dozens of thin strands of nylon twisted together. It comes in a wide array of colors, so it's easy to match this type of thread to a project—the thread disappears into the work. It's best to prepare nylon thread with wax or thread conditioner (see page 78) to prevent it from tangling or fraying.

BRAIDED BEADING THREAD is a material borrowed from the fishing industry. It's made with miniscule synthetic fiber, braided together to make an extremely strong thread. It comes in several "tests," a classification that refers to how many pounds it can hold. The 6-lb. test variety works great for most beadwork projects.

Braided beading thread only comes in white, moss green, and clear, but the limited choice in colors is a small trade-off for such a hearty, nonabrading stringing material. (If you feel you really need to have it all, buy white braided thread and color it with a permanent marker in the color of your choice.) Braided beading thread cuts best with inexpensive craft scissors, not the sharp embroidery kind.

FLEXIBLE BEADING WIRE is made up of twisted strands of stainless steel wire that are coated with nylon. It generally comes in three widths—fine, medium, and heavy—and a wide range of colors, including sterling silver coated and 24-karat gold coated. This wire is not the once-popular "tiger tail" beading wire—it drapes like silk and is resistant to kinks.

OTHER HANDY MATERIALS

When stocking your stash, you'll focus most of your attention on beads, string, and findings. To complete your toolbox, however, you'll still need a few other items.

BEADING MATS are indispensable to have when you're working with seed beads. They keep the beads stable on the work surface so they don't roll around or bounce to the floor. The best type of mat is made with Vellux fabric, but a piece of terry cloth, chamois, or felt works well, too.

GLUES secure beadwork to findings and seal knots. *Industrial-strength clear adhesive* is the strongest glue, but very smelly. Be sure to use it in a well-ventilated area.

Jeweler's or watchmaker's cement is useful for lighter-weight projects and dries clear.

If you only need to seal a knot, you can travel no further than your nail care drawer. *Clear nail polish* works wonders.

WAXES AND THREAD CONDITIONERS are used to pre-coat beading thread. *Beeswax* keeps the thread from fraying and tangling. Some beaders also like the fact that the sticky wax fills up seed beads, stiffening their beadwork.

Microcrystalline wax, a synthetic form of beeswax, works much the same way.

Thread conditioner keeps thread from fraying and tangling, too, but isn't used for stiffening beadwork. Actually, thread conditioner is much like hair conditioner— it makes the thread soft and silky.

TOOLS

Finally, you'll need to have a good set of tools to get the job done. Buying tools is another time to avoid frugality. A good set of tools will yield years of service and few headaches, making them worth the investment.

BEADING NEEDLES generally come in two varieties: English beading needles and sharp needles. *English beading needles* are very thin and come in variable lengths—up to 3" (7.5 cm).

Sharp needles are shorter and thicker than English beading needles. They work great for stitched beadwork because their length makes them easy to maneuver.

Most beadwork projects call for a size 10 to size 13 needle, but needles come in an assortment of sizes. The smaller the number, the thicker the needle.

Scissors are a necessity when creating beadwork with thread. Sharp, pointed *embroidery scissors* work best with projects made with nylon thread.

Children's craft scissors are best for cutting braided beading thread.

Pliers come in a variety of styles, but there are only three that are must-haves for the projects in this book. *Chain-nose pliers* have jaws that are flat on the inside, rounded on the outside, and taper to a point. They're used for making sharp wire bends and grasping and wrapping wire, but also come in handy for pulling beading needles out of a too-full bead.

Crimping pliers have notched jaws used to secure crimp beads and crimp tubes to flexible beading wire (see page 80 for a description of this technique).

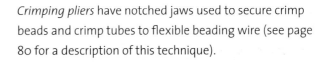

Round-nose pliers have tubular jaws that come to a point and are used for bending wire into curves and loops.

Wire cutters are used to cut metal wire. One side of the cutters makes a flat, or flush cut. The other side makes a V-shaped cut. Buy cutters that are meant for jewelry making only. Those with a pointed tip are usually your best bet. And never use your "good" cutters to cut flexible beading wire—the stainless steel is tough on the blades.

beading know-how

Beadworkers have a wide array of techniques to work with—from simple to complex, functional to experimental. This chapter doesn't include all your choices, of course, but here's a brief guide to the techniques you'll need to know in order to complete the projects in this book.

BEGINNING AND ENDING THREADS

When you have only about 4" (10 cm) of thread left on your needle, tie it off by making a half-hitch or overhand knot between the beads, then pass through a few beads, and pull the thread taut to hide the knot inside a bead. Trim the thread close to the beadwork.

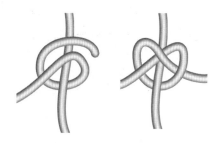

To begin a new thread, pass through a few beads, tie a half-hitch knot between the beads, then pass through a few more beads, and pull the thread taut to hide the knot inside a bead. Trim the tail close to the beadwork.

When you have two thread tails to tie together, use a square knot.

CRIMPING

Working with pliers made especially for this purpose, you'll fold crimp beads or tubes around beading wire to secure the wire to a clasp or connector.

1. String beads to the point where you want to add a clasp. Pass the wire through a crimp bead or tube, through the ring of the clasp, back through the crimp tube, and (if possible) back through a few of the last beads strung.

2. Pull the wire to snug the beads up against the clasp. Making sure the wires are lined up side by side in the tube, use the first (inner) notch of the pliers to squeeze the tube around the wires.

3. Turn the tube on its side and place it into the second (outer) notch of the pliers. Squeeze the tube to form it into a rounded cylinder.

BRICK STITCH

Brick stitch produces a beaded fabric in staggered rows that are stacked in bricklike fashion.

1. Make a base with ladder stitch to the desired length of the piece (see page 84).

2. Exiting from the last bead in the ladder, string two beads and *pass under the loop between the first two beads of the ladder. Pass back up through the second bead just added.

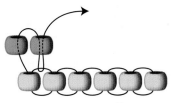

3. String a bead and pass under the next exposed loop between the next two beads. Continue in this manner to the end of the row.

4. To begin the next row, string two beads and repeat from *.

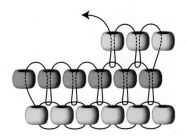

BRICK STITCH INCREASES

To make an end-of-row increase, string one more bead at the beginning of the row and pass through the last loop used once again.

To make a mid-row increase, first reach the spot where you want to make the increase, then string one more bead and pass through the last loop used once again.

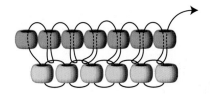

FRINGE

Fringe adds dimension and decorative edge-finishing to your beadwork. You can work with one strand or hundreds, depending on the final look you want.

BRANCH FRINGE

1. String a number of beads for the desired length of the fringe. Skipping the last bead strung, pass back through the beads to the place you want the first branch.

2. String a number of beads for the desired length of the branch. Skipping the last bead strung, pass back through the branch beads and then through the original strand to the place where you want the next branch.

3. Repeat as desired.

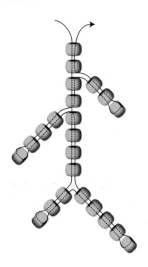

SIMPLE FRINGE

1. Exiting your beadwork base, string the number of beads you want in your fringe. Skipping the last bead, pass back through the remaining beads just added and back into the beadwork base.

2. Repeat as desired.

HERRINGBONE STITCH

Herringbone stitch produces a fabric of beads that looks like multiple two-row columns of beads positioned in V formations.

1. Make a foundation row with ladder stitch (see page 84), using an even number of beads.

2. With the thread exiting up through the last bead of the foundation row, string two beads and pass down through the next bead in the foundation (the second-to-last bead of the row) and up through the bead after that (the third-to-last bead of the row).

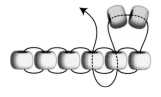

3. *String two beads and pass down through the next bead of the foundation row and up through the following bead. Repeat from * to the end of the row and pass back through the last bead of this row.

4. Continue adding rows by repeating step 3, stringing two beads and passing down and then up through two beads of the previous row.

TUBULAR HERRINGBONE STITCH

This stitch produces a tube that can stand alone, be strung with other elements, or be embellished with fringe.

1. Make a foundation row with ladder stitch (see page 84) that is a multiple of two beads long and either one or two beads high. Join the ends of this foundation row together to form a circle.

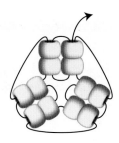

2. *String two beads and pass down through the next bead and up through the following bead. Repeat from * to the end of the round.

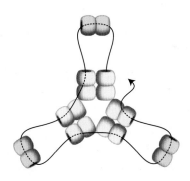

3. At the end of the round, pass through the first bead of the previous and the current round to step up into position to begin the next round.

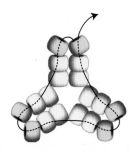

4. When you have finished the tube, tighten and secure the last round by passing through the beads in ladder-stitch fashion (see page 84).

LADDER STITCH

Ladder stitch makes a straight strip of beadwork and is often used to create a foundation row from which to work other stitches. It can be one bead wide or can be made with stacked bead columns.

1. String two beads and pass through both beads again. Adjust the beads so their sides touch.

2. *String one bead and pass through the last bead stitched and this new bead again. Repeat from *, adding one bead at a time, until the strip is your desired length.

LOOMWORK

Loomwork is great for quickly making long strips or large pieces of beaded fabric. The downside is that once you've finished the weaving, you'll have many thread ends to secure and weave back into the work. The threads that are attached to the loom are called warp threads. The threads holding the beads are weft threads.

1. Warp the loom with one more warp thread than the number of beads in the width of your project. Thread a needle with a comfortable length of thread. Leaving a 6" (15 cm) tail to be woven in later, tie the thread to the first warp thread about 6" (15 cm) from the end of the loom.

2. String the beads for the first row of your pattern. Holding the threaded needle, bring these beads under and across the warp threads. Use the index finger of your free hand to push the beads up so there is one bead between each pair of warp threads.

3. Bring the threaded needle over the warp threads and pass back through each bead back to the beginning of the row. Be careful not to pierce any threads as you pass back through the beads.

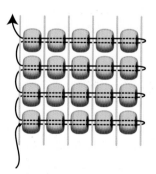

4. Continue adding rows in this manner until you have completed your pattern.

LOOMWORK INCREASES

You can increase only to the number of warp threads available on either side of your main piece, so plan your shaping in advance. You could add warp threads as necessary, but increasing is easier if they are already in place.

To increase at the end of a row, simply add the number of beads desired and finish the row as usual.

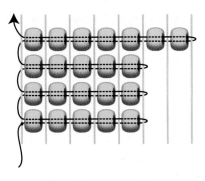

To increase at the beginning of a row, bring the weft thread under, over, then under the warp thread next to the last bead. String the number of beads desired for the increase, push them up between the warp threads, and then bring the weft over the warp thread next to the last bead and through the top of all the increased beads. Pass the thread back under the warp and finish the row as usual, passing through the increased beads again.

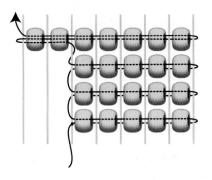

LOOMWORK DECREASES

To decrease at the end of a row, simply string the desired number of beads and bring the weft thread to the top after the warp thread next to the last bead.

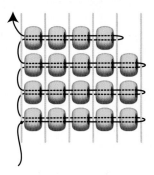

To decrease at the beginning of the row, bring the weft thread under the outer warp thread and pass through the number of beads to be decreased. Bring the weft thread under, over, and under the next warp thread and proceed as usual.

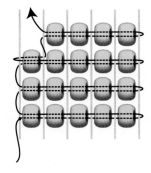

NETTING

Netting can be worked off a base row of beads or a fabric edge. The number of beads and configurations are many, and specific instructions are included with the projects that use it. The final beaded fabric resembles a net.

PEYOTE STITCH

Peyote stitch produces a beaded fabric in staggered rows that are stacked in bricklike fashion.

EVEN-COUNT FLAT PEYOTE STITCH

1. String an even number of beads to the width that you want your piece to be. These beads will form the first two rows.

2. String one bead, skip one bead, and pass through the second-to-last bead of the original beads strung.

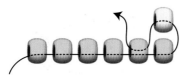

3. *String a bead, skip a bead, and pass through the next bead. Repeat from * to the end of the row.

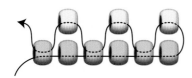

4. Once you have finished this row, every other bead will be sticking up slightly—the "up" beads. On subsequent rows, pick up a bead and pass through the next "up" bead.

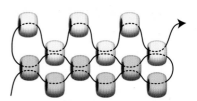

PEYOTE STITCH DECREASES

For a decrease at the beginning of a row, weave through the beads to exit from the spot you want to start the new row and continue stitching. For an end-of-row decrease, simply stop adding beads and begin the new row.

To make a mid-row decrease, stitch to the place where you want to make the decrease, pass the thread through two beads without adding a bead. In the next row, add one bead above the decrease.

Peyote Stitch Increases

When you get to the place where you want to increase, string two beads and pass through the next "up" bead. In the next row, add one bead between the two beads added. You can do this at the end of a row or mid-row.

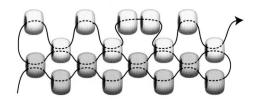

Even-count Tubular Peyote Stitch

1. String an even number of beads for the desired circumference. Pass through all of the beads twice more, pulling the thread tight to form a ring.

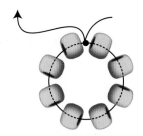

2. *String a bead, skip a bead, and pass through the next bead. Repeat from * to the end of the round.

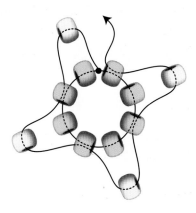

3. At the end of the round, pass through the first bead added in this round to "step up" into position to begin the next round.

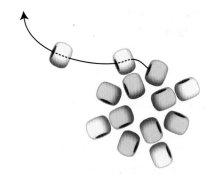

SPIRAL STITCH

This stitch produces a rope of beads, wherein the outer beads spiral around an inner core. You can work with any size beads—just be sure that the outer set is never shorter then the core. This example uses 8° beads for the core and size 11° beads for the outer spiral.

1. String four 8° beads and five 11° beads. Pass through the four core beads again.

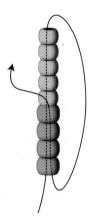

2. String one core bead and five outer beads. Pass through the last three core beads and the core bead just strung.

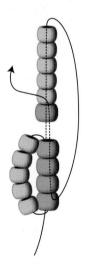

3. Repeat step 2 to desired length.

STRINGING

The most important thing to consider when stringing is pairing your beads with an appropriate stringing material. We recommend specific materials for each project, but in general you should select the strongest material that will fit through the holes in your beads.

Do not try to pick up a bead and put it onto your needle or stringing material. Rather, use your needle or the end of your wire to scoop a bead up from your work surface.

WIREWORK

The topic of wirework could be a book in itself! Here are a few simple wirework techniques that we've used in these projects.

OPENING AND CLOSING LOOPS AND JUMP RINGS

Use two pairs of chain-nose pliers to grasp the ring on either side of the place where the wires meet and gently twist one side up and one side down. Slip your connecting piece onto the loop and close with the reverse motion.

Simple Loop

1. Using chain-nose pliers, make a 90° bend in the wire ⅜" to ½" (1 to 1.5 cm) from the end.

2. With round-nose pliers, grasp the end of the wire. Holding firmly onto the body wire, slowly turn the pliers to form a loop in the end of the wire. Continue turning until the end of the wire meets the body wire.

Wrapped Loop

1. Using chain-nose pliers, make a 90° bend in the wire 2" (5 cm) from the end.

2. With round-nose pliers, grasp the wire at the bend. Use your fingers to wrap the short end of the wire up and over the top of the pliers. Change the pliers' jaw position so the bottom jaw is inside the loop. Swing the short wire end under the bottom jaw.

3. Use your fingers or chain-nose pliers to grasp the short wire end. Wrap the end tightly down the neck of the wire to form several coils.

4. Trim the excess close to the coils.

Wrapping

You can tightly wrap or coil wire to attach one wire to another or to create decorative coils. Start by grasping the base wire tightly in one hand. Hold the wrapping wire with your other hand and make one wrap. Reposition your hands so you can continue to wrap the wire around the base wire, making tight revolutions.

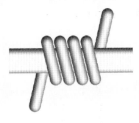

online bead sources

We like to shop at our local bead shops as much as possible—to help ensure that they'll be there when we need them! Here are a few online sources that we also sometimes use.

Artbeads.com > www.artbeads.com

The Bead Goes On > www.beadgoeson.com

The Bead Monkey > www.thebeadmonkey.com

The Beadin' Path > www.beadinpath.com

Beyond Beadery > www.beyondbeadery.com

Bobby Bead > www.bobbybead.com

Caravan Beads, Inc. > www.caravanbeads.com

Cartwright's Sequins > www.ccartwright.com

Dakota Stones > www.dakotastones.com

Fire Mountain Gems and Beads > www.firemountaingems.com

Natural Touch Beads > www.naturaltouchbeads.com

Ornamental Resources, Inc. > www.ornabead.com

Queen Beads > www.queenbeads.com

Rio Grande > www.riogrande.com

Shipwreck Beads > www.shipwreckbeads.com

Soft Flex Company > www.softflexcompany.com

Star's Clasps > www.starsclasps.com

Whole Bead Shop > www.wholebeadshop.com

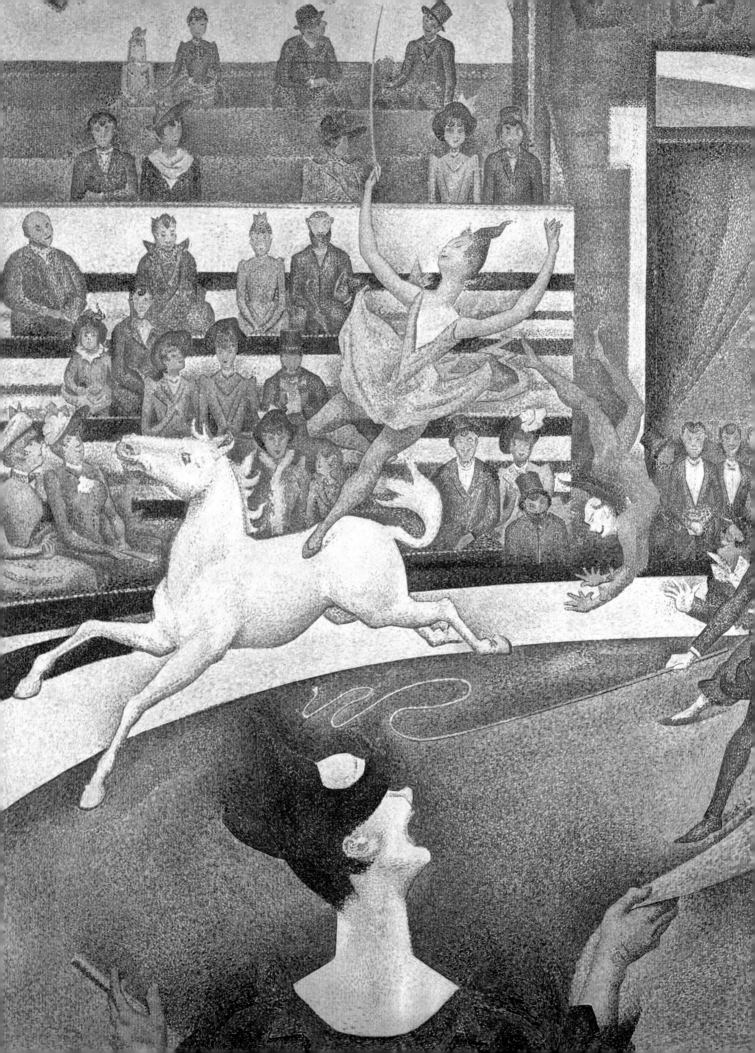

further reading

France, Vernon, ed. *Claude Monet Life and Art*. www.intermonet.com

Gerondeau, Marc. *The Impressionist Movement and Its Greatest Painters*. www.impressionniste.net/impressionism_history.htm

Guggenheim Museum. "Selections from the Collection." www.guggenheimcollection.org

Harden, Mark. *The Artchive*. www.artchive.com

Kelder, Diane. *The Great Book of French Impressionism*. New York: Abbeville Press, 2000.

Mancoff, Debra N. "Landscape with Carriage and Train in the Background by Vincent van Gogh." *Vincent van Gogh Final Paintings*. www. entertainment.howstuffworks.com/vincent-van-gogh-final-paintings18.htm

The Metropolitan Museum of Art. "Childe Hassam (1859–1935)." www.metmuseum.org/toah/hd/hass/hd_hass.htm

MyStudios.com. "Artist Snapshots." Barewalls Interactive Art, Inc. www.mystudios.com

National Gallery of Art. www.nga.gov

Pioch, Nicolas. "WebMuseum, Paris." www.ibiblio.org/wm

Turner, Jane. *From Monet to Cézanne: Late 19th Century French Artists*. New York: St. Martin's Press, 2000.

Vincent van Gogh Gallery: *The Art Information Resource*. www.vangoghgallery.com

Welsh-Ovcharov, Bogomila. *Van Gogh in Provence and Auvers*. Fairfield, Connecticut: Hugh Lauter Levin Associates, 2001.

Weston, Lynley. "Georges Seurat." *University of Michigan School of Information*. www.si.umich.edu/CHICO/Emerson/seurat.html

acknowledgments

Huge thanks go out to all the beaders, designers, authors, and teachers we've encountered over the years—you provide inspiration to keep us going. Thanks to Linda Ligon of Interweave Press for having given us really cool jobs that allowed us to meet each other and advance our beading know-how.

Very special thanks go to Julia S. Pretl, Beading Goddess, whom we were blessed with having as our illustrator and technical editor. Her pictures speak a thousand words. Thanks to the staff at Creative Publishing international, including creative director Rosalind Wanke for providing the guiding light, art director Sylvia McArdle for putting all the pieces together, project manager Ellen Goldstein for directing traffic, and, most especially, editor Deborah Cannarella for encouraging us to get together and write some books.

about the authors

JEAN CAMPBELL is an editor and author with a hankering for beads. She is the founding editor of *Beadwork* magazine and has written and edited more than 40 books, most recently including *The New Beader's Companion* (with Judith Durant) (Interweave, 2005), *Beaded Weddings* (Interweave, 2006), *The Art of Beaded Beads* (Lark, 2006), *Beadwork Creates Jewelry* (Interweave, 2007), and *Beading with Crystals* (Lark, 2007). Jean has appeared on the DIY channel's *Jewelry Making* show, *The Shay Pendray Show*, and PBS's *Beads, Baubles, and Jewels*, where she gives how-to instructions, provides inspiration, and lends crafting advice. She is a certified Precious Metal Clay instructor and teaches off-loom beading and metal clay workshops throughout the United States. She lives with her husband and two children in Minneapolis, Minnesota.

JUDITH DURANT is author of *Ready, Set, Bead* (Creative Publishing international, 2007) and *Never Knit Your Man a Sweater (unless you've got the ring)* (Storey, 2006), editor of *One-Skein Wonders: 101 Yarn Shop Favorites* (Storey, 2006) and *101 Designer One-Skein Wonders* (Storey, 2007), and coauthor (with Jean Campbell) of *The New Beader's Companion* (Interweave, 2005). She is former craft book editor for Interweave Press and has edited dozens of books on beadwork and knitting. She has contributed designs and articles to *Interweave Knits*, *Beadwork*, and *PieceWork* magazines and had a regular column in *Beadwork* for five years. She lives with her husband in Lowell, Massachusetts.